WHISPERING HOPE

WHISPERING HOPE

The True Story
of the Magdalene Women

Nancy Costello, Kathleen Legg, Diane Croghan,
Marie Slattery and Marina Gambold

WRITTEN BY STEVEN O'RIORDAN
AND SUE LEONARD

This edition first published in Great Britain in 2015
by Orion

an imprint of the Orion Publishing Group Ltd
Carmelite House
50 Victoria Embankment
London EC4Y 0DZ
An Hachette UK Company

1 3 5 7 9 10 8 6 4 2

A CIP catalogue record for this book is available
from the British Library.

ISBN: 978 1 4091 6084 7

Typeset by Input Data Services Ltd, Bridgwater, Somerset

Printed and bound by CPI Group (UK) Ltd, Croydon, CR0 4YY

The Orion Publishing Group's policy is to use papers that are natural, renewable and recyclable and made from wood grown in sustainable forests. The logging and manufacturing processes are expected to conform to the environmental regulations of the country of origin.

www.orionbooks.co.uk

On 19 February 2013, the Irish Taoiseach, Enda Kenny apologised in Dáil Éireann to the women who had been incarcerated in Ireland's Magdalene laundries. He promised to put a scheme of compensation in place. A young documentary and film-maker called Steven O'Riordan was there, with some of the women he had helped through his group, Magdalene Survivors Together. *Whispering Hope* tells the harrowing stories of Kathleen, Marina, Nancy, Diane and Marie. It shows how the physical and psychological abuse they endured in various institutions, run on behalf of the state by four different religious orders of nuns, led to a lifetime of shame and secrecy. This heartrending story of suffering and hardship highlights the plight of women in an Ireland dominated by the Catholic Church. Their path towards survival, friendship and hope, as the horrors of past abuse was revealed, typifies the social history of the women of Ireland.

ABOUT THE AUTHORS

Nancy Costello is in her seventies and lives in Galway, helping out a family. Brought up in an orphanage, Nancy attended Magdalene laundries in Cork, Waterford, Limerick and Wexford. She speaks passionately about her experience, happy that, at last, her story is known.

Kathleen Legg, 79, lives in Bournemouth, England. A widow, she has two grown-up children. Aged 14, Kathleen spent three years in St Mary's, Stanhope Street, run by the Religious Sisters of Charity. Officially a training school, it was actually a Magdalene laundry. An intelligent, articulate woman, Kathleen went on to have a good life, but she still suffers frequent nightmares about the time she spent in a Magdalene laundry.

Marina Gambold, 79, lives in Wexford with her husband, William, a retired factory supervisor. At 16, Marina was taken to the Good Shepherd convent in New Ross, Wexford, staying there until she was 19. Marina appeared in the 2010 documentary *The Forgotten Maggies*.

Diane Croghan, 65, lives in Dublin and works in catering. Diane spent three years in the Sisters of Mercy Summerhill Training School, a Magdalene laundry in Wexford, escaping when she was 15. She is separated from her husband, and has eight children, twelve grandchildren and five great-grandchildren. Fiercely independent, she taught herself to read and write, but regrets her lack of a broad education.

Marie Slattery, 56, spent time in the Good Shepherd convent in Sundays Well, Cork, and also in The Sisters of Our Lady of Charity in Sean McDermott Street, Dublin. She then became pregnant and attended a mother and baby home, and was forced to give her baby up for adoption. She hasn't seen her baby since. Marie is estranged from her husband, and their children. She lives in Fermoy, County Cork, and suffers from constant, sometimes crippling, depression.

Steven O'Riordan, 31, is the director/producer of the critically acclaimed documentary *No Limbs, No Limits*, which in April 2014 went on general cinema release throughout Ireland. He also directed the award-winning documentary *Born Lucky* for the BBC and, in 2010, *The Forgotten Maggies* for TG4. He is the founder of the group Magdalene Survivors Together. Originally from Cork, Steven lives in Dublin.

ABOUT THE CO-AUTHOR

Sue Leonard recently co-wrote the number one Irish bestseller *An Act of Love* by Marie Fleming (Hachette Ireland, 2014), about Marie's extraordinary life and her fight for the right to die with dignity. She has worked on three other books as a ghostwriter – two, for Penguin Ireland, were bestsellers. She is the author of *Keys to the Cage* (New Island, 2010). Sue has made her living from freelance journalism for 18 years. She writes interview-based features for the *Irish Independent*, the *Irish Examiner* and many other publications. A former columnist with the *Evening Herald*, she currently writes the 'Beginner's Pluck' book column for the *Irish Examiner*.

CONTENTS

PROLOGUE

IT WAS 19 FEBRUARY 2013, and the Dáil Chamber was packed to bursting. Enda Kenny got to his feet, ready to give a landmark speech. In the public gallery a group of women waited, breathless with excitement. Was their Taoiseach, their head of government, *really* going to talk about them? Women who had been incarcerated in Ireland's Magdalene laundries?

Marina, from the group Magdalene Survivors Together, had travelled to Dublin from Wexford. She could scarcely believe this day had come. When she met the other women outside Dáil Éireann she'd felt overwhelmed with nerves. Who was she to be going into this place of government? Then she spotted Diane from Dublin and the head of the group, Steven O'Riordan, and found herself swept up to the visitors' gallery, and to a reserved seat in the front row.

The chamber was packed, but as Enda Kenny started to talk you could hear a pin drop. She listened nervously, as Kenny said, 'What we discuss here today is your story.' Acknowledging that the women had carried the story, alone, for years, he said,

'From this moment on you need carry it no more. Because today we take it back. Today we acknowledge the role of the state in your ordeal.' Saying these words, his voice broke. He was close to tears.

In the gallery, Marina reached for a tissue. And when he quoted her own words, 'I broke a cup once and had to wear it hanging round my neck for three days,' she clutched Diane's hand and wept openly.

The Taoiseach ended, 'At the conclusion of my discussions with one group of the Magdalene women, one of those present sang "Whispering Hope". A line from that song stays in my mind, "When the dark midnight is over, watch for the breaking of day."

'Let me hope that this day and this debate,' here he paused to compose himself, 'heralds a new dawn for all those who feared that the dark midnight might never end.'

Marina, Diane and the other women, the press and the entire chamber rose to their feet, and clapped their Taoiseach for his brave and sincere words. Then, turning to the public gallery, all the members of Dáil Éireann, from every party, gave the women a standing ovation. Many cheered.

Marina glanced at her friends who were all crying in disbelief. Diane, she noticed, had her arm around a younger woman, who was pale and shaking. 'Diane,' Marina said, 'I can't believe it. The Taoiseach knows we weren't telling lies. He believe *us* and not the nuns.' The applause went on for many minutes before, finally, the TDs – members of the Irish parliament – sat down.

There was one woman missing; a woman who, like Marina, had been involved in the group from the start. It was Kathleen Legg, a survivor who was now living in England. Marina wished she could have been there to share in this precious moment, but she had been unable to fly over because she had cancer. She was in the middle of her radiotherapy treatment.

Steven stood up and beckoned to the women, telling them to follow him down the stairs. Diane introduced Marina to the younger woman. 'This is Marie,' she said. 'She joined the group just recently.'

When the women had walked into the Dáil they had felt awkward and out of place. Now, listening to the comments of 'Fair play to you,' they were the heroines of the hour. Everyone knew they had achieved something miraculous. As they walked towards the plinth outside Dáil Éireann, Marina, Diane and Marie held hands with the others as they revealed themselves to the world.

In Galway, Nancy was watching the women on the news. She couldn't believe her eyes because she too was a Magdalene survivor. It had been her secret and her shame. She laughed with happiness when she heard the women speak. She realised she no longer needed to remember alone.

'We did it,' they said. 'We got justice; we achieved it.'

A shout came from the photographers standing below them. 'Come into the light! We can't see you.'

The media shone lights into their eyes as they stepped forwards. And in turn, they looked out, into the light of the crowd, to the breaking of their new dawn.

CHAPTER 1

STEVEN

WE ALL FELT a sense of triumph on that February day in 2013. I couldn't believe that, after eight years of campaigning for the Magdalene women, the Taoiseach of our country had finally said 'sorry'. The joy shining from Diane's face, from Marina and Marie, was clear to see. I looked at the women with pride. They had done it!

Journalists from all over the world hurled question after question at us, picking me out as the spokesperson and as founder of the Magdalene Survivors Together. After the initial interviews, one journalist took me aside and asked if she could have a bit more of my time. We arranged to meet at nearby Buswells Hotel.

On my way over there, my phone rang. It was Kathleen Legg, the survivor now living in England who had been part of the campaign since the start. 'I saw you Steven,' she said. 'I saw you and Marina on the television news. I heard the apology. I just couldn't believe it.'

'And Stanhope Street was included too,' I said. 'And I

didn't know it would be until I heard Enda Kenny say it.'

I heard her gasp as she realised that, at long last, government officials believed her and not the nuns who had insisted that Stanhope Street was a training school and not a Magdalene laundry. Her voice broke with emotion. 'But that's wonderful,' she said. 'Thank you Steven. Thank you for standing by me and seeing this through. I couldn't be more proud of you if you were my own son.'

I felt humbled as I switched off my phone.

When I reached the hotel I saw the journalist waiting for me in the bar.

'Well Steven,' she said, 'How did a young man like you become involved with the Magdalene women?'

'Well,' I said, laughing. 'It's a long story.'

And it is.

It was 2005 and I was a student at Bath Spa University, England, when my friend, Tim, invited me to watch a DVD of the drama film *The Magdalene Sisters*.

'It's about Irish nuns,' he said. 'They locked up all these women, abused them, and made them work for nothing. It was terrible.'

'Oh yeah?' I said, not really believing him. Tim came from Norfolk and he loved to bash the Irish; it had become a thing with us. A kind of long-standing joke.

We got a Chinese takeaway, cracked open some beers and settled down to watch the film.

I couldn't believe my eyes. Girls were 'imprisoned' in a convent by their families, by the state or by a priest for being too pretty. One was there because she'd been raped. The film showed all these girls, some of them orphans, working all hours in the laundries. The conditions were diabolical. They were beaten if they talked to each other, and some of them had their heads shaved as a punishment. The regime they endured can only be described as slavery.

'Thank God it's all in the past,' I said, 'Thank God the Ireland I know is free and friendly.'

'Yeah, I know. And full of artists and writers and the best pubs in the world,' added Tim, who had heard me praise my country once too often. Sometimes he asked me what I was doing in Bath if Ireland was the paradise I said it was.

'But seriously,' I said. 'If this really happened it must've been in the dark ages, like the Forties, maybe, or the Fifties.' We went on watching, and at the end of the film two of the girls escaped.

'Well thank God for that,' said Tim, helping himself to another bottle of beer. He offered me one, but I waved his hand away, mesmerised by the figures flashing up on the screen. This film, I realised, was entirely based on fact. Over 30,000 women had passed through the doors of Magdalene laundries since the first one was set up in 1765. And the last one closed its doors in 1996. 1996? That had to be wrong. I was 12 then; surely I would have known? But I didn't. So much for Ireland being the land of saints and scholars.

I didn't sleep that night. I lay there thinking about those women. And of how Irish people like me, known for our thousand welcomes, had allowed this degrading inhumane treatment of our own citizens to happen. Surely this could not be true? Could the film-makers have got it all wrong?

I knew that in the past Irish women had got a raw deal. When John Charles McQuaid was head of the Church in Ireland there was no worse sin than being unmarried and pregnant. Sex was simply taboo. In fact, people often joked that there was no sex in Ireland before Gay Byrne brought it up on *The Late Late Show*.

Intrigued, I Googled and discovered that the Magdalene laundries started as a good Christian idea. An institution on Dublin's Upper Leeson Street gave over 100 destitute women food, clothes, shelter and a place of work, the agenda being to get them off the streets.

When, after expansion, there weren't enough prostitutes to run the laundries the nuns took in 'fallen women' – as they termed unmarried mothers. And then orphans were sent there, fresh from industrial schools, and people with deformities or learning disabilities. Anyone who could be forced to work was welcome, it seemed. The laundries became an important source of income to the nuns, and more institutions popped up around Ireland as the Church encouraged hotels and hospitals to send their laundry there. Ultimately Magdalene laundries became big business, rather than a safe haven for women.

The records for the laundries are incomplete; but in the years between 1922 and 1996, when there are records for almost half the women, only 16.4 per cent went there of their own free will. The others were placed there by their families, by priests and by state agencies.

Four religious orders were involved. They were the Religious Sisters of Charity, the Congregation of the Sisters of Mercy, the Sisters of our Lady of Charity of Refuge and the Sisters of the Good Shepherd. 'Homes' operated in Cork, Limerick, Waterford, Wexford, Galway and Dublin. The last woman was admitted as recently as 1991.

I felt angry with the film-maker for leaving the story where he did. Didn't he care what had happened to those 30,000 women? I started to wonder how many of them had got out. And did they manage to pick up the pieces and lead normal lives afterwards? Had they families of their own? Were they happy?

I wanted to find out more, and I wanted to help. So I wrote numerous letters to government representatives in Ireland, asking them to address the issue and to help the Magdalene women, but my letters were ignored. I returned home to Cork when I graduated from Bath Spa in 2006. I thought, I am going to bring these women into the media. I'm going to get their stories told.

I had qualified as a producer/director and decided to make a documentary on the women who had come out of the laundries, to highlight what had happened to them since. Anything to bring them back to public attention. I thought it would be easy, but it proved difficult to find any survivors, let alone to get any funding.

Then I discovered that a developer had bought the site of a former Magdalene laundry in Dublin's High Park, back in 1993, and had been given permission to exhume 133 bodies – the number the nuns said were there. Once the exhumation started they stumbled upon 22 more bodies and had to apply for another exhumation licence, which was issued by the Department of the Environment. They gave permission to exhume all the human remains, which caused upset because we will never fully know how many women's remains were in the grave. Some of the women had no death certificates, and other death certificates were incomplete. Some of the women had broken wrist, ankle, elbow and leg bones, and one of the women had been exhumed without a skull.

The order of nuns said they knew nothing about it. Nobody seemed to know who the women were, or why they died at this institution. I felt I had to get to the bottom of this.

I visited laundry buildings throughout Ireland. Many had mass graves. Were they the norm? The large Victorian asylums once dominated the cities' skylines, but they now stood in ruins, isolated and overshadowed by an ever-growing multicultural, progressive society. Barbed wire covered the tops of the walls, while enormous steel railings stretched from corner to corner, enclosing the extraordinarily dead, sad landscape of falling down, neglected convents.

Walking round each, I could sense an atmosphere of hurt, loneliness, shame and secrecy. Holy statues lay abandoned, overgrown with brambles and weeds. It was hard to imagine the girls trapped here and labouring. I scoured the neighbourhoods, chatting to people who might unlock the mystery, but nobody seemed willing to talk. Were the survivors really lost to memory?

When the laundries finally closed, some of the Magdalene women were so institutionalised they were unable to live independently. Today, they still live in institutions operated by the state run by nuns. In 2007 I visited one hoping to talk to the inmates, but the nuns refused me entry and called the Gardaí.

I eventually met some of the women who were ending their days in an institution in Cork. I'd hoped they would tell me their stories, but they were silent, looking in on themselves.

One woman, Janet, sat in a chair all day holding a mirror. Every few minutes she would pick it up and look at herself. Smiling, she would say, 'Amn't I beautiful.'

I looked at her straggly grey hair, her wrinkled face and sad, defeated eyes, and told her that yes, she was beautiful.

I asked the nurse about her and she said, 'They didn't have mirrors in the laundries. The nuns felt that would encourage vanity. And vanity was a sin. Janet never saw her own face once she had gone into the laundry, and she went in at 15.'

That story broke my heart.

In 1991, when the last woman was admitted to a laundry,

Ireland had its first female president in Mary Robinson. Roddy Doyle's film *The Commitments* was showing a hip modern Ireland. When, in 1994, Riverdance exploded onto the world stage leading to the belief that everything Irish was great, there were *still* women enslaved in the laundries. I just couldn't get my head around it.

As the months passed, I started to contact all the religious orders who ran these homes, but none of them would allow access to any woman who had been in their care. Their line was 'We need to protect the women'. I simply could not understand why these women had no free will? I ploughed on. I signed up to numerous forums and looked at endless websites, but I couldn't find a single Magdalene survivor willing to speak to me.

All the time I was hitting these brick walls, I carried on with my research. And everything I read showed that the film, *The Magdalene Sisters,* had portrayed things reasonably accurately. Comparively few girls went to the laundries because they were pregnant. A huge number were there because they'd been raped or abused by members of their families. Some, like one girl in the movie, had indeed been placed there because, being pretty, they were seen as a temptation to men. Huge numbers were orphans. Some had disabilities or learning difficulties. They had nowhere else to go, and that's why they ended up slaving in the laundries.

I did, eventually, find a few Magdalene women – a couple were willing to appear in my documentary but others didn't want to, and needed emotional support. I tried to raise finance, but the Arts Council refused me funding; my friends, clearly fed up with my obsession, stopped listening. I didn't drive and had run out of people willing to ferry me around. I was about to jack in the whole thing. My parents were thrilled.

'Thank God you've seen sense Steven,' they said. 'Now you can get yourself a job.'

Then I remembered Elaine Hooper, a local youth worker I knew, who I felt just might be interested in what I was trying to do. I rang her, and she listened to me and agreed to help. We decided to go to Limerick and visit a Magdalene survivor there.

We met Sadie, who had asked us to meet her in a cemetery where a number of Magdalene women were buried in a mass grave. She had brought a couple of friends along with her, and we stood there chatting. She told us her story. She was working in a hostel in Dublin when she was approached by two members of the Catholic organisation, The Legion of Mary. She thought she was getting a paid job, but ended up in a laundry working for nothing. She was there for three or four years. We were talking about the women in the mass grave. She said, 'It's awful. Nobody knows how they died, or what had happened to them.' I asked if it was known how many women were buried there and she said over 300. She said there was a campaign to get the nuns to release the names of the women. I looked at the size of the grave compared to others I had seen. 'I feel there are many more women here,' I said. 'Perhaps they should be exhumed.'

I can't explain this next bit but, as I stood there, I felt an overwhelming sense of energy coming out of the grave. It was as if the women were actually trying to dig themselves out; as if they were saying, 'Help me.' I just had this strong image of these women coming up through the earth, seeing their fingers grasping at the soil before their hollowed out faces were revealed. It was so powerful. So horrible. I felt these dead women wanted to say, 'Our story hasn't been told.'

Sadie left. I turned to Elaine. 'I have this weird sense that these women want me to tell their stories.' I described what I was feeling, expecting her to laugh. But she said, 'Steven, I felt the exact same. It was really eerie, and creepy.'

'Well if you felt that, and I felt that, we really do have to do something about it.'

Elaine agreed.

Sadie didn't want to be in my documentary, so I thought I would try further afield. I contacted a number of societies in the UK which had been set up to help and support Magdalene women. I spoke to Phyllis Morgan of the London Irish Centre in Camden. She was a survivor of an institution. She told me her story, and put me in touch with a number of women who lived in the UK. And that is how I first met Kathleen Legg.

CHAPTER 2

KATHLEEN

EVERY DAY WHEN I wake up I think I am back at St Mary's, Stanhope Street. My alarm clock peals and I panic, thinking, 'I must get up quickly. I must wash. I mustn't be late for chapel.' Then I open my eyes and I'm in my bedroom in Bournemouth. The sun is shining through the curtains, sending a beam of light onto the ceiling. I sink back on my pillows, and my racing heartbeat starts to slow.

For 60 years I kept a secret. I had never told anyone that I was once in a Magdalene laundry. Not a soul. I never even told my husband. We were married for 38 years and I never breathed a word of it.

After he died, though, I began to think more about that time. The scandals about the Catholic Church were starting to come to light, and I realised that I shouldn't be feeling such overwhelming shame. And the year after he died, I heard that a Review Board was being set up in Ireland to look into all the institutions run by the Catholic Church. I met Phyllis Morgan, who was the head of the London Irish Centre; she had been abused by the nuns too.

I decided it was time to tell my story, but it wasn't easy. I wondered, would she think I was lying? Or would she presume I had been a so-called 'fallen woman'? The nuns had done a good job of destroying my confidence and making me feel that I deserved the treatment they meted out, and I thought she would blame me too.

I said all this to her, and she took my hand between hers and said that whatever I told her, she would believe me. And she did. She sat there with tears in her eyes, and when I cried she didn't comment. She just passed me a tissue. She believed every word, and the burden I had carried for years lifted.

It was she who put me in touch with Steven O'Riordan. And that meeting changed my life forever.

I didn't have a promising start in life. I was born in the county home in Limerick, on 7 October 1935. My mother stayed there with me for two years. She wasn't married. That made her a fallen woman, and I was considered 'devil spawn'. When I was three years old, Mammy took me to a home outside Tipperary town that was run by the Presentation Nuns.

I had my first ever memory there. I'm playing peek-a-boo, hiding under a sheet and popping out, and a child across this big room is laughing. There were so many beds in that room that they went all round the walls, and down the middle too.

The rest of that time is a blur. My mother never would talk about it. When I asked her about my birth and childhood, she said, 'That's in the past.' I think it was too painful for her to remember, but I wish I had pressed her more. I imagine she had to work for the nuns as she would not have had the money to pay them for looking after me.

I can't be sure, but I think she was working in the laundry. One time I was screaming my head off, and a nun gave me a spoonful of sugar. That soon shut me up!

When I was three, Mammy took me to live with my grandparents in Lisvernane in County Tipperary, where my grandfather's sawmills were. My Uncle Mikie lived there too. She then left to work in Dublin, which was about 120 miles away. She came to see me once a year, and stayed just a day or two, but I didn't love her and she didn't love me either. Half the time she called me a bloody nuisance.

I loved my granny. She always wore black, and had a black shawl tied around her shoulders. When she went to Mass, she put it over her head. Women had to cover their head in church back then.

We had to look smart for Sunday Mass. On Saturday night, Granny washed my hair and set out my best clothes. In summer, Mass was the only time we wore shoes, though in winter I had boys' boots and thick stockings. I knitted the stockings myself.

The village school was just across the road. I could run home for lunch. The farmer's children had to stay in school to eat their sandwiches and drink their bottle of milk. They had a long walk to and from school, as they lived up the mountainside. When it was raining and cold, they'd arrive shivering and soaked to the skin.

It was a tiny school with just two classrooms, a junior and a senior. We learned to write with a slate and a piece of chalk, and then used pens that you dipped into an inkwell. If you weren't careful you'd leave ink blotches everywhere and you'd get a slap across the face. The teacher wore a large ring and I got cut by it more than once. She'd strike me across my ear too.

The worst times were when Auntie Katie came to stay. My

mother's sister, she came from England with her husband, Paddy Gleeson. They hadn't any children, and she hated the sight of me.

One day, when I was five, I didn't want to go to school. 'I want to stay with Granny,' I said, hanging on to her apron. Granny just smiled, but Aunt Katie raised her eyebrows.

'Come here,' she said, and yanked me, roughly, by the hair. 'You *will* go to school.' She slapped me hard. Then she dragged me across the road, beating me all the way. Our neighbour was outside sweeping her front steps. She stared across at me, but said nothing. Nobody did. Everyone who was out on the street just stood and watched.

After school, instead of leaving with my best friend Mary, taking the time to share secrets, I dawdled home – anything to see less of Aunt Katie. But that gave her another excuse to hit me. One day, she grabbed me as soon as I stepped through the door.

'You're late Kathleen,' she said, whacking me. 'I needed some messages. Where were you?'

'We were kept back . . .' I said, but she wasn't listening.

'Don't answer back.' She was screaming, her face red with temper, her eyes bulging. Dragging me round to the side of the cottage, she laid into me. It's like a devil had taken her over. She hurt me so much, but I didn't cry. I wouldn't. That made her crosser. She hit me harder and harder and harder. I thought she'd kill me.

Then there was a shout. 'Hey Katie love. Katie. Stop that now!'

It was Paddy Gleeson, Katie's husband. I've never been so pleased to see anyone. He pulled her off me, and I lay there, dazed and battered.

'She's a divil that one,' said Katie, trying to escape her

husband's clutches as she kicked out at me. 'She deserves everything she gets.'

People in the village must have known what she was doing to me, but nobody tried to help. What happened inside families was not seen as anyone else's business. There were often fights in the street when the men came out of the pub. I expect their wives got a clatter when they got home. It was just part of life.

The priest turned a blind eye to violence. He didn't seem to care about our welfare. All that mattered to him was that you went to Mass on Sundays, and took the sacraments of confession and communion.

Life was very basic. The cottage had a mud floor. Granny swept it with a besom – twigs tied to a long handle. We lived in the one room. My grandad had made all the furniture, the table, chairs and the bench. There were two bedrooms downstairs, one for my grandad, the other for my granny and me, Uncle Mikie used a ladder to get to his in the attic.

I loved my granny so much. I loved knowing she was always there, in the kitchen, looking after us all. I loved watching her baking, the kitchen warm with steam. I loved sleeping in the bed with her, hearing her breathing beside me. It made me feel safe.

Granny cooked on an open fire. Grandad brought down wooden chips from the saw mill, and stacked them in the corner of the yard. We ate pig's head with vegetables, and bread and apple pies which were baked in the fire.

One Wednesday, when I was 11, Granny didn't get up. I wondered why. Nobody said she was ill, and I don't think she saw a doctor. But when I got home from school on the Thursday, my mother was there. Auntie Katie arrived from London the following day. The two of them kept whispering.

I lay in bed in the second loft room, where they had sent me to sleep, trying to hear what they were talking about downstairs. Then I dropped off, and the next thing my uncle was shaking me awake.

'You had better come into your grandmother's room,' he said.

I walked in and saw my mother and Auntie Katie on their knees. My uncle told me to kneel down too. We said prayers. I didn't know why. Then I was sent back to bed.

The next morning Mammy gave me some money. 'Could you go up to the shop please, Kathleen?'

'What about school?'

She looked at me strangely. 'You think we'd send you on a day like this?'

I shrugged. What was she talking about?

'Go to the shop and get some black stockings will you? Get some for Auntie Katie and me, and some for yourself. Can you do that?'

'Of course.' I skipped off. As I made my way up the village, happy to be free, I noticed people staring at me. And when I asked for the stockings the shopkeeper said, 'I'm sorry for your trouble.' I stared at her, thinking, *That's odd*. I had absolutely no idea what she was talking about.

The woman from next door came in to wash Granny, and then these two stern men in black suits arrived with a coffin. Grandad said, 'Kathleen, you had better come in and kiss your grandmother.' I did that. I didn't feel scared. I suppose I now knew she was dead. I *must* have known, but I felt numb. And, odd though it is, I still didn't understand that I would never see the only person I really loved again. It just didn't sink in.

After that, the car came for the coffin and took it the short distance to the church. Grandad, my Uncle Mikie and all the men from the village followed the coffin to the church for the removal, but women weren't allowed to attend back then. We stayed behind in the kitchen, making piles and piles of sandwiches.

At about six that evening I sneaked out of the house and went up the road and into the church. The closed coffin had flowers on it. I took some petals and put them in my prayer book. Going home I started to sob, and once I'd started I couldn't stop because I finally realised that Granny had gone.

My mother held my hand as we walked to church the next day for the funeral Mass; then the men hefted the coffin into the graveyard. I tried to follow to say goodbye to Granny, but Mammy pulled me home. 'The graveyard is no place for women,' she said.

And soon after, Mammy went back to Dublin and I stayed on with Grandad and Uncle Mikie. That wasn't ideal. There I was, soon to enter my teens, with all the changes happening to my body, and my emotions, being looked after by two men. Although, in truth, I more or less looked after myself.

'You can sleep back in Granny's bed now,' said Grandad that first night. It felt so strange lying there, in that wooden planked bed with the straw mattress. I could hear mice squeaking and I worried that one would bite me. I missed Granny so much. What would I do without her? I cried, silently, into my pillow, hoping that Grandad wouldn't hear.

Outside my bedroom the floor was alive with beetles. I was terrified of stepping on them. When I did, there'd be a crunch, and I'd scream in fright.

There were lice in the cottage too. My red hair came down to my waist, and I'd lie in bed feeling my hair moving. Sweet Jesus, I hated that! I'd hang my head out of the bed, because then I couldn't feel the lice anymore. Grandad hadn't a clue how to deal with them, and neither had my uncle. They decided it needed a woman's touch, and took me next door but one, to where my friend Mary lived with her family.

'Could you comb Kathleen's hair please,' he'd say to Mary's mother, and she'd smile, and sit me down in the kitchen. She would tut at the state of my hair. 'Would you not let me cut it Kathleen?' she'd say. 'There are that many knots and tangles, and however often you come over here, we never can get rid of these pesky insects.'

But I shook my head. I was proud of my hair.

After Granny died, I took over some of the chores. I'd sweep the floor and collect the water. I'd run down the street, lined on either side with cottages, until it opened up to a field. I'd climb over the stile and across the field to the well which supplied the whole village. Staggering home with the heavy buckets, I'd feel sorry for the women who lived at the top of the village, because they had to lug their buckets all the way up the hill.

I had never much liked school. But I hated it once I moved into the senior classroom. Our grey-haired teacher, Paddy Lynch, was old and close to retirement, and he made my life hell.

I don't know why he didn't like me; it was probably because I was 'a bastard', or maybe it was my height. When I was about to leave school, at 14, I was five foot eight inches tall, and he was about five foot, so I could look down on him. I'd say he hated that.

At roll call in the morning he'd call everyone else by their names, but when he came to me he'd shout out, 'Is telegraph pole here?'

All the children would giggle behind their hands, and look round at me, and I would blush beetroot red. Paddy Lynch would smile smugly, loving my discomfit. He'd mock me with the nickname all day. It was humiliating and cruel, and he knew that.

Mr Lynch made me his skivvy. Larry O'Donnell and I had to stack the turf in the shed, and I had to arrive early each morning to lay the fire and light it with paraffin and matches. If it wasn't roaring by the time Paddy Lynch arrived, he'd give me hell all day.

The one person who supported me was my friend Mary. 'You should tell your Grandad,' she said, flicking her plaits behind her shoulders. So I did, but he didn't listen.

'Paddy Lynch is a God-fearing man, Kathleen. I won't have you speaking ill of him.'

'But it's not just me. He hits us all!'

'He does? Well then, I'm sure you all deserve it.'

That wasn't fair. We didn't. If somebody made a mistake in their catechism he would punish us all. He'd make us hold out our hands, and he'd come along the row, lashing every one of us with a stick. He smiled as he did this. I'd say he got pleasure from it.

Yet he was known as a good religious man. And he loved nothing better than to drum the catechism into us. It was the only thing on his mind. He'd have taught it from morning until home time if he could.

The summer holidays were my respite. We'd all go into the woods at the back of the village to pick whorts, which were like blueberries. The woods were full of them. We'd wander through, the dappled sunlight illuminating the woodland floor. It rained sometimes, but the trees protected us from the worst of the wet. Sometimes we'd ping back a branch and shower each other with raindrops. We worked hard, because we'd get paid three shillings and sixpence per bucket. That was great money! I'd plan what sweets I was going to buy, but Uncle

Mikie would watch out for me coming home and would ask for the money.

'What would *you* need it for?' he'd say, as he counted the coins. 'You'll only waste it and ruin your teeth.'

That was so unfair. Because I knew that *he* would spend it on porter and Woodbine cigarettes. I did feel sorry for him though, because Grandad never paid him a proper wage. He had to beg for every penny.

But how I missed my sweets! When Granny was alive she would give me a halfpenny or a penny for sweets, but that all stopped when she died. Mammy never gave me money. I might get a small box of jelly babies when she visited, and at Christmas she sent a colouring book and some crayons. That had to do me.

There were good, happy days though. Days I would spend with Mary. We'd walk in the woods, talking, and we loved to go down to the river to swim. It was so peaceful there, listening to the babbling of the water over the stones. We'd wear our vests and pants pinned together. Those were carefree days, but my childhood was soon to end.

CHAPTER 3

KATHLEEN

ONE DAY IN late August, 1949, Mary and I were sitting by the river dangling our toes in the water. Mary was picking grass, nervously. She was being sent to a boarding school, and she didn't want to go one bit.

'You're so lucky to be staying here,' she said.

I just shrugged because now that I was almost 14, I knew that I wouldn't be going back to the school. I didn't like the idea of slaving for Grandad and Uncle Mikey all day, and I was worried too because Grandad had told me another uncle was going to live in the cottage with him, and his new wife was coming too. I couldn't think how we would all fit in.

It was getting dark when we got up to wander home, and the air was crisp with an early hint of autumn. We skipped up the village street, anxious to get in to the warmth. Mary shouted goodbye and I ran the last few yards, bursting through the front door and into the kitchen. 'We've had a lovely time,' I shouted, then I stopped dead. Mammy was sitting there with Grandad. And she wasn't smiling.

'There you are,' she said, turning to me. 'You need to get your things together, we're leaving.'

'Leaving? Leaving the village?'

'You're coming with me to Dublin.'

'With you? But why?'

Mammy looked at Grandad, but he just turned away. 'There's nothing for you here now,' she said. 'It's time you got a training.'

'A training? What sort of a training?'

'A training for a job,' she said.

'Do we have to leave right now?'

She nodded.

'Can I go and tell Mary?'

'Haven't you seen her all day?'

'But I can't go without saying goodbye.'

'Quick then. We've a bus to catch.'

It was hard saying goodbye to Grandad. Harder still to leave the cottage with all its memories of Granny. It took over five hours to get to Dublin, and I brooded as I stared out of the bus window, watching the lights of the villages we passed through. I had a big knot in my stomach. What was going to happen to me, and how would I manage with my new life?

My mother said she had found somewhere for me to go. 'I was talking to my landlady, and she told me that there's a convent down the road where they take girls in for training.'

I was wondering how Mammy would pay for it. Mary had heard her parents say that her boarding convent school would cost them a fortune. Then she said, 'Sometimes, they take girls without payment.'

I nodded.

'It's called St Mary's. If the nuns will take you, it will set you up for a job.'

That sounded okay to me – I really enjoyed my education and was eager to learn more.

As we walked for my interview, I was feeling more excited than nervous. But when we turned into Stanhope Street, and I saw the dark forbidding building – which looked almost sinister with its small windows twinkling in the sun – I felt a sense of foreboding. Could I be happy living somewhere so very much bigger than the cottage I was used to? St Mary's was bigger than the church in the village; bigger even than the hospital in Tipperary where I had gone to have my eyes checked over.

We walked up to the massive oak door and rang the bell. It opened to reveal a tiny nun with glasses, who wore a black habit from head to toe. My mother explained that we were expected, and I smiled nervously, but she scowled back and, without a word, showed us into a massive hall with highly polished floors and an arched ceiling.

We sat down for a while. I stared round at all the holy statutes and fidgeted, nervously. I was hoping I would make a good impression because I wanted to continue with my education. Then we were shown into a parlour. It was Sister Fidelis's office. She stood up when we walked in. She was tall, the same height as me, and she seemed surprised, and maybe a little annoyed, that I wasn't smaller. She scowled as she looked me in the eye, and grunted to herself, but once we had all taken our seats she talked, and handed my mother a list of all the things I would need.

'Do you sing, Kathleen?'

I jumped. Then stammered out, 'Yes. Yes I do.'

'That's good,' she said, and actually smiled. 'Sister Brigid will be delighted to hear that. You will be useful for her choir.'

Maybe this wasn't going to be so bad after all. I thought, maybe this is a chance for a new start – a proper future.

I stayed with my mother in her bedsit while we prepared for my new life at St Mary's. We spent the week shopping in Cork Street for cotton dresses, nightgowns, flannels, soap, and a toothbrush and paste. I'd never had a toothbrush before. In the cottage we'd rubbed salt or soot on our teeth with our fingers. As the day got nearer for my enrolment I became more and more excited. I was thrilled to be starting on this new adventure. What a naive girl I was.

CHAPTER 4

KATHLEEN

I WAS NERVOUS the following week when my mother shook my hand and left me on the doorstep of St Mary's and in the care of the Sisters of Charity. I didn't know when I would see her again, but I hadn't time to think because Sister Fidelis appeared and whisked me away.

'Come, follow me,' she said, leading me up the stairs to a huge dormitory on the top floor where I was to leave my things. It was remarkable how small a bag all my worldly possessions could fit into. Then Sister Fidelis handed me a kind of pinafore to wear over my cotton dress, and she told me to put it on immediately. Then it was down the stairs again and along a corridor, before she opened a door, beckoning me in.

I had been expecting to see a row of desks and a teacher at the end of the room, but I was in for a shock. There wasn't a desk in sight! I turned to Sister Fidelis, feeling puzzled. I was about to ask where the classroom was when a huge billow of steam engulfed us, the wet, intense heat almost overpowering. It was hard to breath, and my words were lost.

The steam cleared to reveal an enormous room jam-packed with 20 or 30 children my own age and large, ominous-looking machinery. Every child was handling sheets while singing a hymn. A few looked round when they saw me, but they were swiftly commanded to keep working.

This, I was to learn, was the calendar room. The calendar was a roller iron. It was a vicious machine, like a road roller, and was about nine feet wide. Two girls had to feed wet sheets into it but there was no safety guard. It would snatch the sheets from your hands, so there was a real danger that your fingers might get caught. I remember the hiss as the steam from the wet sheets rose. By the time they had finished the sheets were bone dry, and ready for yet more girls to fold them.

'Kathleen, you can help prepare the wet sheets for the calendar,' said Sister Fidelis, pointing to these huge canvas baskets on wheels. I watched the other girls as they hauled the sheets out, trying to untangle them without letting them drop on the floor. It was clear you needed real strength for the job. Sister Fidelis left the room and I gingerly walked over to the girls sorting the sheets and said, 'Hello.'

They looked terrified, and put their hand to their lips to indicate silence. I was confused. We weren't allowed to talk while we worked? I suppose that's why they all sung hymns. It was better than working in silence.

I joined them, and leaned over to pull out a sheet. It had sounded such a simple job, but the weight of the sheet made it an exhausting one. Using all my strength, I pulled the sheet backwards. It broke free suddenly sending me falling onto my back on the floor, the sheet on top of me. I expected the other girls to make fun of me, but they remained stony faced.

Luckily the sheet hadn't hit the floor, so once I'd untangled it, I leaned over to put it in the machine. Then one of the girls shouted, 'Watch your hair!' I stood bolt upright in shock. It hadn't occurred to me, but there was a real danger that our long hair would get caught in the calendar. It gave me such a fright, realising how easily I could have burned my head, that it was hard to concentrate for the rest of the day.

After three hours or so, we were called down to supper. We ate in a cavernous dining room, sitting round long tables in silence. That felt so strange. I longed to talk to the girls, to make friends and find out more about life in the school. I noticed many were very thin, and they looked pale. But the worst thing was that nobody smiled. They looked defeated.

There were a few older women at the tables. They ate in silence too, and later I would notice them as we all went about our work. I wondered what they were doing in a training school.

I cried myself to sleep that first night, but I didn't make a sound. There were so many girls in that dormitory. The bed was rock hard, so that, however I shifted myself around, I could not get comfortable. My back ached unbearably. It was a while before I dropped off. I thought of my grandmother and of how close we had been. I wondered if anyone would ever love me again.

CHAPTER 5

KATHLEEN

I WOKE ABRUPTLY to the sound of a bell. Forcing my eyes open, I noticed a nun marching up and down, and my heart sank.

'Out of bed,' she said, clapping her hands for attention. 'All of you. On your knees.' She began to pray and all the girls joined in, so I did too.

That first day, I tried to follow what the other girls did. They were rushing to wash in the washroom, and to dress. I put on my underclothes, then took off my nightgown, and there was a scream from the nun.

'You! You new girl. Have you no modesty?'

I looked around and noticed that the other girls had put on all their clothes under their nightgowns. I blushed, wanting to disappear through a hole in the ground.

We combed our hair quickly, but couldn't see what we looked like because, as I was soon to discover, mirrors weren't allowed in St Mary's.

We went to Mass in the chapel before breakfast. It was

divided into three parts by high partitions. We were sectioned off on the right side with the nuns in the centre while anyone from the outside sat on the left side. Clearly the nuns didn't want us mixing with the outside world.

I was starving that first day, as I lined up with the other girls outside the refectory. When the nun opened the door, we rushed in and the girls went straight to their marked cubby hole where they collected their cutlery and an apron. A cubby hole was assigned for me.

Sometimes we had sausages, but more often breakfast was a large spoonful of porridge. Then we had a small roll with a pat of butter. There was stale bread left on the tables too, for anyone hungry enough to have it. I was surprised how many girls ate it. I longed to talk to the others, to find out what to expect next, but we weren't allowed to talk at mealtimes either. A nun sat up on a pulpit reading from a prayer book.

The next time a bell rang – a hand bell this time – the girls got up and fetched a bowl of water. Then they washed up at the table. I did the same. Then another bell rang and we had to go and do some housework.

I found the next hour, between 8 and 9 a.m., exhausting. We had to scrub and polish floors so that between us we left the whole building, the rooms and the corridors, gleaming. By the time the bell rang at nine, summoning us to our places of work, I felt as tired as if my whole day's work was done.

The first few days passed in a haze of prayer, meals and hard, hard work. I wondered when our lessons would start. This was a training school for young ladies, wasn't it? But I soon realised there was no school. This was it. Just the hard grind. Part of me just accepted that. What other choice did I have? This, I thought, must be normal life.

I had always been shy, and had never found it easy to make

friends, but here, where friendships were not only discouraged, but with our enforced silence not even possible, I found life unbearably lonely. I missed the camaraderie of school, though I never, ever missed Paddy Lynch.

I was put back in the calendar room where I worked for the first few months. There were three of those horrible machines in that room. Four girls were assigned to each machine, with another two to each for folding the sheets. It was like a military operation, and we were like robots, working with our heads down, rarely daring to speak.

I was terrified of the calendar. The steel roller and sheet of metal underneath it were red hot. I was always worried I would get burned when the jaws grasped for the sheets. It happened to us all, so often. I had been there a week when I got my first burn. I watched my skin blister and, trying not to cry from the pain, went to find Sister Vianney, the nun in charge, hoping for some first aid and sympathy.

'What are you doing here?' she asked, then gave my hand a cursory glance. 'That'll heal in time,' she said, shooing me back to work.

Sister Vianney was the nun in charge of the room. She didn't sit there all the time, a nice woman from outside supervised us, but whenever there was a problem you could be sure she would appear. Sometimes the sheets got caught and the calendar jammed. We had to pull down a switch to release the sheet. This took a minute or two; we always tried to rush through it, hoping Sister Vianney wouldn't notice. But she invariably did.

No sooner would the switch be released than she'd come bustling in, all five foot nothing of her, shouting at us all and calling us idiots.

'Do you realise how time-wasting that is?' she'd say, her face getting redder and redder the angrier she got. 'Time is money girls. You must *not* fall behind.'

Her double chins would wobble as she spoke. We hated her.

A bell would ring at 11 a.m. for a break. By that time we'd been working solidly for four hours and would already be exhausted from the endless grind. We would go to this bare room, with benches and cupboards, most with their doors hanging off and a few half broken chairs. It was called the playroom, but I don't think any play had ever been done in that dismal room. We'd have cocoa and stale bread and margarine, and the same at 3 p.m. It would be 20 minutes break, exactly.

Lunch was back in the refectory, with the same routine as at breakfast; queue outside, collect our cutlery and apron, eat in silence while a nun read and wash up afterwards. We had potatoes and cabbage – always cabbage – with a tiny piece of fatty meat. This every day except for Wednesday which was 'dessert day'. This was either bread-and-butter pudding, rice pudding or rather runny thin custard. The snag was that desert was instead of our usual savoury lunch, and *not* as well as it.

Still, *anything* was better than cabbage. I hated it so much, and had to force it down. One day I left a spoonful. I covered it with my fork, hoping to get away with it, but Sister Fidelis saw and started roaring at me.

'How dare you leave your food, Kathleen. Eat that cabbage right now!'

'I can't sister. I feel sick,' I said. It was the truth. But she made me sit there until my plate was clear. I was there for an hour, long after all the other girls had left the dining room. But when the bell pealed summoning us back to work, I forced the cabbage down. I felt sick but, knowing Fidelis would be back to check on me, I didn't dare defy her. She had won, as she always did.

We had a glass of water with lunch, but even so we all got very thirsty in the steamy heat of the calendar room. It had a glass roof, so in summer it became unbearably hot. Whenever anyone went out to the toilet, they would take this metal bowl with them – like a dog bowl. They would bring it back full of water, and this would be passed around to everyone. It was undignified, and we only had one sip each, but it was better than nothing, and we would do *anything* to quench our thirst.

Tea was at 5 p.m. That was stale bread with margarine and jam, and a cup of tea. After that, we had nothing at all until 7.30 the next morning. The first week I felt hungry all the time. And I mean *really* hungry, with a constant ache of emptiness that kept me awake at night.

Slowly my stomach started to adjust but I became very thin. I could feel my ribs in bed at night, and then my hip bones started to jut out. My arms and legs looked like sticks, and the thinner I got, the more my strength left me.

One morning after breakfast, we were told to queue up so that Sister Frances Bernadine could dispense glasses of medicine from her walk-in cupboard. I waited for my turn, and drank the white chalky liquid. I nearly gagged on it.

'What is this for Sister?' I asked, forcing myself to swallow.

'Never you mind. Any more words, and you can have some more.'

I ran off in case she carried out her threat, but I did wonder what it could possibly be. A few hours later I noticed a girl in the laundry hold her stomach in pain. She asked if she could go to the toilet. A few minutes later another girl asked.

It was almost lunchtime when my stomach started to cramp. I bent over double in pain and realised that I too needed the toilet in a hurry. Clearly we had all been dosed with a laxative. This rigmarole happened every month that I stayed in that place. I have absolutely no idea why they would do that, but I thought of it as a form of torture.

My periods stopped altogether. I didn't have even one in the three years I was there, nor for years afterwards. It was a relief to be free of the monthly bleeding and stomach cramps, but it worried me too. Was I not going to be a normal woman?

After tea, it was off to chapel, then at 6 p.m. we were free, if you can call it freedom when we couldn't get beyond the high walls that bordered the grounds. We were, anyway, too exhausted to do anything much with our spare time. We would sit slumped in the playroom, or perhaps go for a walk outside, and then bed was at nine. We'd line up round the stairs, all 54 of us, in two rows. The most senior girl, Nellie Mangan, was number 1 and my number was 26. The sister on duty would stand there in her long black habit, her arms folded in front of her as she shouted out our numbers. I gradually lost the sense of who I was.

We would go to the wash room, which had small sinks all the way round but only cold water. We took it in turns to collect hot water in big jugs from a bathroom along the corridor, which we poured into the basins. We'd wash before getting undressed under our nightgowns. Then we'd kneel by the bed for prayers, dictated by a nun who would walk the length of the dormitory. Then it was lights out. And the cycle would start again.

CHAPTER 6

KATHLEEN

I SOON BECAME used to the routine. When the bell rang I knew exactly where I had to go, and started walking in the right direction, queuing up with the others. We walked slowly with our heads bent. We weren't allowed to talk, and after a while I don't think we wanted to. We didn't become friends. Friendships were never encouraged, and we were all so very frightened of the nuns.

They were never violent; they didn't have to be when they had such absolute power over us. It was the mental cruelty – and their total disregard for our welfare – that made us hate them so much,

One day, I was walking down the draughty corridor on my way to the toilet when Sister Fidelis beckoned me into the playroom. Sister Frances Bernadine was sitting in there holding a cup of tea. I waited by the door to find out what they wanted from me, but they acted as if I wasn't there. I was so confused.

'She's a strange one, this Kathleen,' Sister Fidelis said, looking not at me but at the other nun.

'She's tall though. That should make her strong and handy for the work,' Sister Frances Bernadine replied. And I smiled to myself, thinking, maybe she is jealous, because she is so small and dumpy.

'But she's nothing to say for herself,' said Fidelis.

I didn't reply, sensing a trap. How could I have anything to say for myself, when we weren't allowed to talk?

'Very quiet,' continued Fidelis, prodding me with a finger between my protruding ribs. 'Bony too.'

They laughed, as I blushed, not knowing where to look.

'Agh, the quiet ones are always the worst.' This was Sister Frances Bernadine.

'That they are.' They stopped talking and eyeballed me. 'Well?'

I cocked my head, not sure what to say.

'Haven't you work to be getting to, Kathleen?'

'Yes Sister. Of course Sister,' I said, and scuttled out, leaving their mocking laughter behind.

I never knew why they called me in there, but that happened almost every week. Maybe it was because I had a free place and my mother was unmarried. Most girls were there because their parents or guardian paid a fee. Or perhaps they called all the girls in from time to time, but if so, nobody ever mentioned it.

Sister Fidelis was in charge of the domestic side of things; she supervised the cleaning and the running of the kitchen. Sister Frances Bernadine was supposed to be in charge of our welfare. Well, with barely enough food to keep us going through the day, that was a joke!

I think those two nuns were evil. I feel quite sure they got a lot of pleasure from taunting and tormenting me. They knew they could say whatever they liked about you, and you had no comeback. I wonder, did they think I was arrogant and needed pulling down a peg or two? Maybe my height gave me the appearance of confidence? I really don't know. What I *do* know is that I was scared rigid of them. I have never got over that sense of a loss of self they instilled in me. They made it clear that to them I was worth less than nothing.

My mother, to give her her due, didn't just abandon me there. At the start she appeared every month. She would bring me a little cake which I would share with the girls who sat at my table. After a while, though, even that small pleasure was stopped.

Sister Vianney came to get me from work, one day, telling me that my mother was waiting for me in the parlour. But as I was making my way down the corridor she called me back.

'Kathleen – a word,' she said. I stopped and turned. 'Could you tell your mother she can't come in any more?'

'Oh! Yes,' I stammered. 'Yes Sister.' I felt flustered. Had she done something to anger the nuns? And if so, how could I tell her without hurting her feelings? I waited, expecting Sister Vianney to explain, but, her message delivered, she strode down the corridor.

Looking back, I'm pretty sure I know the reason. Even though my mother never stayed long – we usually spoke for just ten minutes – it took another five minutes for me to get to the parlour to see her, and to get back to work again. In that time, someone would have to stand in for me in the calendar room, and that meant precious minutes of work time would be lost. That would really have got to her.

Mammy did still come in occasionally, just once or twice a year. But I could tell even this concession bothered the nuns. I was never allowed more than 10 minutes or so with her, and we were never left alone. There would always be a nun hovering, listening to every word.

Once a year my mother would come and collect me to take me back to the village for a few days. She never asked me what went on at St Mary's, even though she must surely have noticed how much weight I'd lost.

I never told her the truth. We weren't close, and I suppose I wanted her to believe that she had done her best for me. I didn't know it then, but my mother was receiving reports from the nuns which gave the impression we had lessons and exams in physical culture, needlework, cookery, housewifery and conduct. We got a mark for laundry, too, but there was no indication, none at all, that we spent our days slaving for the nuns.

I would see Mary when I went home. It was wonderful roaming around the village and through the woods with her – like being a child again. She didn't talk about her convent boarding school, and I never told her the truth about the laundry. I knew she was sitting at a desk at school, learning her lessons, and I was jealous. We hadn't a clue about each other's lives.

My days at home were all too brief. No sooner had I got used to breathing fresh air and eating well, and it was back to the drudgery. That first year, sitting with my mother on the bus, I wondered whether to tell her something of my life. I was thinking about it, trying to work out what words to use, when Mammy said, 'Isn't it lucky we found St Mary's?'

'*Lucky?*' Was she joking?

I sighed, and wondered had I got it wrong? Were all training schools like St Mary's, and was it me not being able to fit in? I kept silent, but started feeling sick at the idea of returning for yet more 'training'. And as soon as we rang that front door bell at St Mary's, the minute I entered to that perpetual smell of damp mixed with polish, I felt as if I had never been away.

*

On my return from Lisvernane, I was put to work in the sewing room, turning the collars of the priest's shirts and patching sheets. This work was as tedious and relentless as any other. My eyes would ache by the end of the day. We were never granted any slack.

Add on the hour of cleaning, and we were doing more than an adult's normal work but for no wage at all. We worked five-and-a-half days a week, and girls without parents only had Christmas Day and St Stephen's Day off each year.

Time meant nothing to us. We kept track on which day of the week it was and, obviously, with the dismal Irish climate we knew the seasons but, with nothing to look forward to, and no change to our routine, the months slid by. Our birthdays were never celebrated, so we weren't even sure of our age. Little by little, every sense of who we were before entering St Mary's was washed away.

We kept that place spotless. We would be allocated different parts of the convent to clean and I spent several months in the chapel, along with a live-in lady – one of a twin who had arrived together. Along with the large area of floor, we had to polish the choir gallery and clean the sacristy, the corridor and the porches. The corridor was lined with floor to ceiling cupboards, and these were full of candlesticks and other altar brass. This, of course, had to be cleaned as well.

I don't know why, because no outsiders ever came in. I knew that because after six months or so I was moved to work at reception. There was a big huge door in the reception area, and a black shiny phone on the wall. There was a bell too, and every nun had a code. You'd ring one-one-two for the Reverend Mother and one-one-two-three for Sister Fidelis, and so on. When they heard their own particular code sounding on the gong, they would know to come out of chapel.

I had to clean all the parlours, but then it was just a question of sitting in the office waiting for the phone to ring or the doorbell to go. It wasn't such a bad job, except that I worked there until 9 p.m. I'd be sitting there wishing I was with all the others in the playroom.

From there, I went to work in the kitchen. The kitchen work was overseen by Sister Fidelis, but she was more concerned with the administration. She decided on the menu and served the food in the refectory, but we did all the cooking and the cleaning in the kitchen. It was tempting to steal food, but in spite of the aching hunger we never did. The nuns had sewn seeds of distrust between us. We knew that if another girl saw us with food she would tell the nuns.

I never once met the Reverend Mother, not in the whole three years I was there. She stayed firmly in the nuns' quarters. She didn't even visit us on Christmas Day. This left Sister Fidelis and Sister Frances Bernadine wielding absolute power.

I often wondered why no local people came through that door. A priest came in of course, there was one who was a director of St Mary's so he must have known exactly what was going on. And the doctor who occasionally appeared must surely have suspected that the regime was harsh, but no school inspector ever appeared. Neither did any government minister.

And that is really odd. Because I now know that the state paid the nuns a fee to have some of the girls there. I believe that the government knew about the place, but turned a blind eye to the goings on. The convent was doing them a service.

Among the general public, though, nobody knew what was happening behind that door. Everyone assumed St Mary's was a training school; they didn't know that us girls had any connection with a laundry. That might sound unlikely, but the laundry was at the back of the convent and the vans carrying the linen would drive all the way round to the entrance at the back.

The nuns were great at portraying the best side of the so-called school to the public by putting us on show. On Saturdays, before tea, we had to wash our hair – usually in cold water – and we'd be inspected for lice. I remember holding my breath, praying that the nun in charge didn't find anything.

Sunday was the only day that we wore our official school uniform, which in winter was a black tunic with a hand-knitted, pale blue jumper. We were allocated these when we first arrived. They would be handed down from girl to girl to save the nuns money. In the summer we wore blue-checked cotton dresses. The uniform would be laid out on Saturday night.

In the morning there was Mass, then after lunch we were sent out for a walk. We wore our berets, which had the school badge on the front. We had to line up down the corridor to be inspected. It was vital that the school badge should be straight.

'We can't have you letting down the school,' was the constant mantra. I realise, now, that it was imperative for the nuns that the locals had a good impression of us.

We'd hear, 'Look! There are those school children looking all neat.'

We would wander up to the Phoenix Park, and just walk around for a few hours. We'd climb the steps of the monument, and sit around listlessly on the grass. Then we'd go back and have our tea.

One day this young man on the street recognised Maureen, one of the girls at St Mary's, and he came up to talk to us. It turned out he was her cousin. Somehow that got back to the nuns, and we were all made to kneel for an hour and listen while Fidelis lectured us about the dangers of talking to men around the town.

The door to the outside was never locked; we could have

walked out of the gates easily if we had wanted to, but while I was there nobody ever did. Where would we have gone? We were so passive. Terrified of the nuns, we just accepted our lives, assuming they were normal.

But one Saturday night I woke up and saw a black shape at the end of my bed. I thought it must be Sister Fidelis and I dropped back to sleep, but every time I opened my eyes she was still there. Later other girls woke up and started screaming. The figure turned out to be a man who had escaped from the nearby Grangegorman mental asylum and had walked through the open door. He had taken a gymslip from someone's chair, and had draped it over his head. There was pandemonium! The nuns called the men in white coats but nobody came to see if we were all right.

I didn't think too much about the incident at the time, but later in my life I started to have nightmares about a man in black at the foot of my bed. I still have nightmares about him, even today.

The nuns referred to St Mary's as an orphanage, yet few of the girls were actual orphans. Even so, we were invited to a performance of a pantomime every Christmas, put on for 'the poor orphans of Dublin'. A highlight was when the actors, who had given up their time for free, came round the audience handing out a bag of sweets for each of us.

Christmas Day was marked at St Mary's but it was not happy. There was no Christmas tree, ever, but there was a crib. We were woken up for midnight Mass and we went to church again in the morning. After dinner, we were taken to this big room upstairs to line up and get our presents.

A priest dressed as Father Christmas would hand out the parcels. We'd hope for some chocolate, or notebook and pen, but every year it was something practical like a face flannel and a piece of soap, which wasn't much reward for 52 weeks of slave labour. One year when my name was called out I went up to the priest, but he deliberately dropped my parcel. He didn't apologise. I bent down to pick it up and he hissed, 'You were the one who dropped the potatoes.'

I was mortified. It's true that some weeks earlier, working in the kitchens, I *had* dropped a tray of potatoes. My hands were burning from the steam. My arm was badly burned, but nobody cared about that. All that mattered was that the potatoes were alright, that little damage was done to them. The girl in charge took them into the dining room to be served.

But why had the incident been brought up again, and on a day that was supposed to be a celebration? Sister Fidelis was behind it all. When she saw what the priest had done, she roared with laughter, and all the other children joined in.

At least that time nothing had been broken, because breakages at St Mary's were taken extremely seriously. I broke a glass once, and another time the top of a hot water bottle used for one of the elderly residents who lived at the convent because they couldn't care for themselves. Us children had to pay, which as we were never paid a penny for our labours wasn't easy. I had to ask my mother for the money as they were making me pay for a whole new hot water bottle. That was so unjust! Mammy sighed when I asked her, and I felt such guilt, knowing she didn't have money to spare.

There were younger girls who lived in a different part of the convent and went to school. Sometimes I envied them. I really missed my education, but they didn't have it easy. Even the smallest ones had to do an hour's cleaning before school, and afterwards they would be sent to the sewing room for an hour.

I'd feel for them when they came into the laundry to collect the priest's socks, to check them for holes and darn the ones that needed it. It was one thing to work *us* to the bone; using such young children really was child slavery.

CHAPTER 7

KATHLEEN

ONE MORNING I woke up shivering with cold. I pulled the blanket higher around my shoulders but it made no difference. I wriggled, trying to get comfortable, but that was never easy when the bed dipped so dramatically in the middle. My back was always sore after the day's labour in the laundry, but that morning my neck felt stiff too. I moved my shoulders in an attempt to loosen it, but my head felt locked in place.

As we dressed that morning, our breath distilled into the cold air. I felt faint at Mass, and felt myself sway, but I didn't collapse as some girls often did. I got through the service somehow. I couldn't eat any breakfast, and polishing the floor I yearned to curl up into a ball and expire.

By the time we went down to the laundry I couldn't think straight. Dying of thirst, I asked to go to the toilet and took the bowl to fill with water. In the corridor I met Sister Frances Bernadine.

'Look at your face, child!'

I put my hands to my cheeks. They were burning and clammy under my cool palms.

'It's the mumps,' she said, dragging me by the arm. 'I'd better get you away before all the girls get it. You're the second this week – and we can't afford to lose any more.'

She half marched, half dragged me to a small room well away from the main building. Another girl was already in one of the two beds that practically filled the room. I got into the other and dozed for a while. It was ironic, I thought, that at last here I was able to rest for once, but my head spun horribly so I couldn't enjoy this welcome break.

At lunchtime Sister Fidelis appeared and plonked down a tray with two plates on it. Each plate contained a small potato and a tiny portion of cabbage. Feeling sick I pushed my plate away, but she didn't say a word. She didn't even ask us how we were, and we didn't see her again until tea time. When she came to collect that untouched tray she turned out the lights.

For the first few days I felt very sick, but we never saw a doctor. Sister Fidelis gave us lozenges to help our throats, but that was the only treatment we received. No kindness was on offer either. Nobody came near us except at mealtimes, and if we had needed help during the night there was nobody to turn to, and probably nobody who would have heard us call. There wasn't even a bell.

When we began to feel a little better, boredom took over. There were no books to read; nothing at all to do, and we were lonely, left there on our own. There wasn't a clock, so mealtimes were the only way we measured time. That made the days drag even more.

You'd think we'd have made friends, but we were so cowed by the nuns that we didn't speak much at all. I was naturally quiet, and she was even shyer than me.

With all this time to reflect, my thoughts drifted to questions about my father – I wondered who he could have been. I had asked Mammy about him – of course I had – but she was always vague. 'He didn't want to know,' was all she would say. But suppose she was wrong? What if he now yearned to know his daughter, and didn't know how to find me? *Maybe*, I thought, *he will turn up one day and rescue me from this place.*

After 10 days or so, when we were pronounced better, it was straight back to work. The nuns always assumed that my height gave me extra strength, but the truth was that I was always frail. I constantly felt exhausted during my time at St Mary's, and a few months after I'd got over the mumps I woke feeling particularly weak. I went through that day in a daze. Nobody commented, or suggested I should rest, but after the working day was over an older girl approached me and said, 'Your mother is here.'

I was surprised. She rarely came, but I went into the parlour and there she was. The little bag I had arrived with was there beside her.

'Are you ready Kathleen?' she asked.

I was confused. 'Where are we going?'

'To the hospital of course.'

'The hospital?'

'The nuns tell me you're sick.'

So they *had* noticed. Why, then, had I been made to work?

My mother and I walked all the way to Dr Steevens' Hospital. I remember it so well, walking by the quays, listening to the screaming of the seagulls, and watching the passers by rushing home from work. Meanwhile my brain felt like a fog – my head was spinning, and I was finding it increasingly difficult to put one foot in front of the other. When finally we arrived, the doctor took one look at me and got me into bed in a ward. I had pleurisy.

'That's what killed your grandmother,' said Mammy, which did nothing to raise my spirits.

When they accepted me at the convent, the Sisters of Charity became my guardians and were in charge of my welfare. Yet no charity was ever on offer. The first sign of serious illness and they contact my mother. But they were the ones who were working me into an early grave.

Sister Fidelis and Sister Frances Bernadine came in every single day to visit me, though not out of concern for my well-being, I'm sure. Perhaps it was out of a sense of guilt or duty. Or did they simply want to taunt me? They always came empty handed. I was made to sit up in bed, ramrod straight, with my hands folded on the sheet. This was difficult, because I was very sick. When I sat, my head spun with dizziness. All I wanted to do was lie back and sleep.

They sat either side of the bed and talked away, though never to me. It was all gossip relayed across me, about the convent, the penitents and the news of the day. One time, they were going on about a politician called Noel Browne. They called him an antichrist and said he was in favour of fallen women.

'Paying penitents who are selfish enough to hang on to their babies? I've heard it all now,' said Fidelis, as Frances Bernadine pursed her lips in disapproval. 'He's a terrible man altogether.'

'Ah, Archbishop John Charles McQuaid will soon put him back in his box,' said Frances Bernadine.

And strange as it may seem, the Archbishop of Dublin did just that. Browne's radical proposals were so hated by the Church, and the Church had so much power back then, that they brought down the government in the end.

I'm not sure how long I was in hospital; two weeks maybe,

but when I was better my mother appeared and we made that long walk back to Stanhope Street. Now that I felt relatively well the walk back was much easier, but I dragged my feet, anxious to delay the moment of arrival. Mammy left me on the doorstep before Sister Fidelis opened the door. She let me in, greeting me with a shout of glee.

'Ah Kathleen! You're better now I see.'

'Much better, thanks,' I said. 'Though the doctors say it will be a while before my chest is quite clear.'

Sister hadn't heard that last bit. Or if she had, she had decided to ignore it. She was sweeping along the corridor, indicating that I should follow her. She opened the door to the kitchen and said, 'The shirker is back!'

Nobody referred to my illness again. But it had changed me in an unexpected way. I can't say that I had enjoyed being in hospital – nobody likes being ill – but I had felt at home in that atmosphere of caring. I had watched the nurses as they bustled around the ward dispensing drugs and making beds, and I envied their ability to care for us all. I began to wonder if, one day, I might become a nurse.

There was a woman in the convent called Jane – one of a few older women who, for some reason, couldn't live independently. I don't know what her background was, but she was blind, deaf and dumb. She would spend most of her day in the kitchen, and was always there for her meals. I put the plate on a small table in front of her, and I would put her knife and fork into her hands.

Jane had soft white hair worn in a bun, and her cheeks dimpled when she smiled. She wasn't always easy, and when she was frustrated she would throw things around. Other girls were scared of her, but I loved her. She reminded me of my grandmother. To me, she *was* Granny. Seeing her each day gave a focus to my life in St Mary's. She was the first person I had been able to care for in a practical way, so she helped me to learn my strengths in life. I still think of her and it makes me cry each time that I do. Jane lived down a corridor in a cubicle alongside the other older women.

One of these women was a Miss McMahon. She had a hunched back and she worked in the sewing room. I was fond of her too. Both women brought out a softer side to Sister Fidelis. She was especially nice to Jane, taking care over her; washing and dressing her in the morning, and taking her to the toilet, and undressing her at night.

I found that confusing. I had become so used to despising Fidelis, with her small mean eyes, but the contrast made the cruelty of her behaviour towards all of us children even harder to accept.

It wasn't long before the nuns saw signs in me that I would be a suitable person to become a nurse – and could therefore work for them when my so-called training finished. As the winter of 1951 set in, Jane caught a cough and it didn't go away. The hacking sound echoed around the kitchen. She'd sit there, breathless and in distress, with tears pouring down her cheeks.

One day, when I put her lunch in front of her, Jane accepted it meekly, but then refused to eat. I tried to feed her, but she spat the food back out again. I felt her forehead and it was burning. I told Fidelis. She took one look and said, 'It must've gone to her chest,' and between us we helped her up to bed.

I was chosen along with another girl to sit beside her. It was heartbreaking watching her as day by day her condition worsened. We did what we could for her, sponging her body in an attempt to bring down her fever, but it was useless. I don't think she even knew we were there.

One day, Jane's bed was empty, and I realised she had died. I don't remember anyone actually telling me that she had. Her death wasn't referred to, but the day she'd gone I saw two strange men in the corridor, and I realise now that they must have been undertakers. I was so sad at her death – it was like my granny dying all over again. Without her, the days in the laundry seemed to stretch to infinity. I felt lonelier than ever inside those grim walls. I missed her so much, and I still do.

Most girls stayed in St Mary's until they were 16. After that, they left – mostly to other employment, but the nuns had their eye on me to work in another of their institutions, so I stayed on a third year until I was 17. That year dragged. I couldn't wait to leave. I muttered as much to a girl working alongside me in the kitchens.

'Only two more days left in this house!' I said. 'And it's all I can bear. If I have to spend an extra night here, I think I'll die.'

She laughed. But either I was overheard, or she reported me to the nuns, because after work Sister Frances Bernadine grabbed me and took me into the main parlour, where all our documents were kept. She handed me a formal-looking piece of paper. I stared at it and saw that it was my birth certificate. I'd never seen it before and hadn't a clue what her giving it to me meant.

'You do know, Kathleen, that I can keep you here? I can detain you for life if I want to.'

'But—'

'You can live in the corridor with all the other older workers,' she said, referring to the corridor where Jane had lived. I knew this was no idle threat. There were several older woman workers. 'The Reverend Mother has the authority. So, do you want to thank me for training you ready for your nursing career?'

I was flabbergasted, but did so. I'd have said anything to get out of there. And leave, I did.

CHAPTER 8

KATHLEEN

AFTER THREE YEARS of gruelling work, I was thrilled to see the back of St Mary's. As the door shut behind me on that January day in 1953, I took a deep breath of fresh air. I felt that at last my life was changing, and for the better. I was ecstatic to be going the few miles to St Patrick's Infant Dietetic Hospital in Blackrock, Dublin. I couldn't wait to start my training as a nursery nurse. It was something I had dreamed of.

I left that laundry without even the money for the bus fare, my mother had to supply me with that. She came with me, and was impressed with the imposing entrance and long driveway at the hospital – as was I. She settled me into my small room in the nurse's home and left.

First I was handed my uniform – a dress with an apron, and a white starched square that was to be a butterfly hat.

'My goodness you're tall,' said the apple-cheeked nun staring up at me. And when I put the dress on, I was shocked at the way it hung off me, emphasising the amount of weight I had lost at St Mary's. Back in my room, I attempted to make my hat. It wasn't easy – I was all thumbs – but in the end I was happy enough with my effort.

I couldn't sleep that night for excitement, and I couldn't eat any breakfast either. I arrived on the little girls' ward to find it strangely silent. The children lay in cots around the square, bare ward and didn't make a sound. I'd expected a warm welcome from a ward sister, but there was just another girl there, of about my own age.

'Hello,' she said, smiling. 'I'm Annie. Welcome to St Patrick's.'

I smiled back but she was running off, saying over her shoulder, 'We'd better get to it.'

'Yes?'

'Breakfast for the children,' she said. 'Out of their cots, into highchairs, bibs on – you get the picture.'

I wasn't used to handling small children, but by watching Annie I managed as best I could. I was thinking, *Soon I'll get some instruction*. But we never did. We were just left to get on with it, though a nun would occasionally stand in the doorway and watch us for a minute or two.

I liked Annie. She was pretty with soft brown eyes, her fair hair pulled into a ponytail, and we worked well together. But that first morning passed in a blur of business, as we rushed to get through the routine with the toddlers and small children.

There was one thing that bothered me. This was a hospital, but the children didn't appear to be ill. I asked Annie what was wrong with the children, and she looked at me strangely.

'What do you mean?' she said.

'I just wondered why they are all in hospital.'

She just shrugged and muttered, 'You'll see soon enough.'

The second day I was there, Annie said, 'Could you give me a hand getting this one dressed up.' She indicated a small girl of about two or three years old. Annie and I dressed her in a pretty dress, frilled socks and a pair of little shoes.

'Why have they given her such pretty clothes?' I asked.

Annie laughed. 'She's off to America. Only the best for her.'

'She is very pretty,' I said, noticing her fair curls and bright blue eyes. 'But why is she going to America?'

Annie shrugged. 'I supposed they've found some parents for her there. Anyway, it's lucky for her!'

'Lucky?'

'They only want the fair, pretty ones.'

When she was ready, Sister Mary came in and inspected the girl. Checking that we had washed her behind her ears, and that her fingernails were clean and clipped, she whipped her away. 'Right,' she said. 'Off to the priests with you.'

'The priests?'

'To take her on the plane,' said Sister Mary. 'She's been chosen by a very special family.'

I felt sorry for the little girl travelling all that way with a priest. I wondered why the family hadn't come to collect the child themselves if they were so keen to adopt her.

I soon learned that St Patrick's was no more a real hospital than St Mary's was a training school. There were no visitors and nobody from outside ever questioned what was going on there. It was actually a home for illegitimate children like me, who I well knew were considered nothing but a burden on the state, being the children of 'fallen women.' The children came straight here after they had left the mother and baby homes. I suppose it was a sort of business.

At the time I didn't think too much about that. The Church was so strong back then that I accepted it as being just the way things were – just as I had presumed that slaving in the laundry was normal.

It's only recently, when all the scandals have come out, that

I've realised how wrong the whole transaction was. The nuns would have been paid good money for every child they sent. And many of the mothers, who gave birth in a nearby mother and baby home, would have been forced to give up their babies. Some of them hadn't even signed the papers. It has caused so much heartbreak over the years. It causes me distress to think I was part of that process, however unwittingly.

After a while I just accepted that the children were here, and that I was to care for them. I wish I could say that we loved those children and treated them as a mother would, but we didn't. Not really. We didn't know how. Or at least I didn't.

I had never been hugged as a child, and I hadn't seen affection shown to any children by their parents. We did keep those children clean, and we gave them basic care. We were kind to them, but that was as far as it went. We hadn't any time to play with them or to cuddle them.

Yet we *did h*ave time to polish their shoes. This was the last duty we performed as day staff, and it came after the children's tea, when they were tucked up in their night clothes, and all the lights were out.

It must have been a harsh life for the children. The smaller ones only came out of their cots for meals, and I don't remember seeing any toys. Some of the older children were taken around in pushchairs occasionally, but I was never given that task.

We worked hard at St Patrick's. There were just two of us on duty for around 20 children. We'd be up at 7 a.m., and would have our breakfast before arriving on the wards at eight. We'd find the children already dressed, waiting for their breakfast to arrive. We'd sit them down with their bibs on, and would have to spoon-feed many of the children their porridge.

The nun on duty would come and check that all was well,

then it was off to the potty room. The children had to sit there on their potties until they had performed. This might take an hour. That can't have been right, but we knew no better, and were used to simply doing what we were told. It was unthinkable to challenge the nuns.

When we'd taken the children off the potties, we'd put them back into their cots, where they'd just sit or lie down quietly. They had no toys yet they rarely cried. They didn't speak either. Meanwhile we had to pull all the cots out so we could clean around them; then push them back and scrub the centre of the floor. After lunch they went back into their cots, leaving us to mend their clothes.

I enjoyed my stint in the baby's ward upstairs. There was a little girl who had water on her brain. I was very fond of her, and I liked it that she seemed to recognise me, making a small grunting sound as she looked at me through unfocused eyes. She was a dead weight with her enlarged head, and it was terrible strain having to lift her in and out of the bath.

I think of her sometimes, and wonder what happened to her afterwards. There is no chance that she would have been adopted, so I suppose, if she survived, she would have been transferred to an orphanage.

I would meet my mother on my precious day off. One day, showing me into her bedsit, she looked nervous.

'Are you alright?' I asked, as she wrung her hands together.

'Of course,' she said, avoiding my eye. 'But Kathleen, I have something to tell you.'

My heart was beating fast. I thought, *At last! She's going to tell me who my father is.* I had been badgering her about him for years but, as much as I would ask her that, she never would tell me.

'I'm getting married,' she said.

'Oh.' It was all I could think of to say. She was 39 years old, and to me that seemed ancient. 'Um, who to?' I didn't know she was having a romance.

'He's called Joe. And he's a very kind man,' she said. 'I think you'll like him.'

And I thought to myself, *Well, as long as* you *like him. That's what matters.*

'The wedding is next Wednesday,' she said. 'I do hope you can come.'

I had the day off anyway, but knew I would be late back. So I went to the nun in charge and told her I was going to a wedding.

'That's nice,' she said. 'And whose wedding would that be?'

'My mother's,' I said, blushing scarlet, because for some reason I felt ashamed of that.

I met Joe at my mother's landlady's house, and I liked him at once. Almost as tall as my mother, he had a round friendly face, and he laughed readily. He made me feel immediately comfortable, and I understood why Mammy liked him so much.

The landlady's daughter was acting as bridesmaid, and someone from Joe's work was best man. The four of us were carefree as we walked to the church. We walked in together, and the priest approached our group. Then, ignoring my mother, he walked straight up to her bridesmaid.

'Would you come up to the altar with your intended,' he said. We hastily explained and the priest apologised for his mistake.

It was a happy day, and I felt closer to my mother than I had perhaps ever felt before. Watching her smile at Joe during the service, and seeing how happy she was with him at lunch afterwards, I began to see life from her point of view.

It can't have been easy having an illegitimate child. While I don't think she always acted in my interest, I could see that life hadn't been all roses for her either. And I began to realise that she did care for me a little – certainly she wanted the best for me.

I was happy working at St Patrick's. I liked the work and felt settled in the routine. Nursing was something I felt suited to, and I was confident that I did it well. So when, after seven months, my mother arrived and told me she had come to collect me because I was leaving, it came as a terrible shock.

'What have I done wrong?'

'Wrong? Nothing. But you're not strong Kathleen. Your weak chest worries the nuns – and especially that time you had pleurisy. They can't keep employing someone who is likely to be sick at the drop of a hat.'

'Where are we going?' I asked.

'We're going to Stanhope Street,' she said.

CHAPTER 9

KATHLEEN

'WHAT?' I SAID to Mammy. 'You're taking me to Stanhope Street? You're handing me back to Sister Fidelis?' I sat down in shock, my head spinning. She couldn't mean it – could she?

My mother shook her head. 'Not as such. We're going there so that Sister Fidelis can introduce you to your new employer.

'New employer?'

'That's right Kathleen. The nuns say they've found a job for you as a housekeeper.'

'But I want to stay at St Patrick's,' I said. 'I'm getting stronger all the time. I can manage, I know I can. Besides, they owe me some wages.' We got paid the grand sum of £1 a week.

'Housekeeping is a grand job,' she said. 'I should know. I've done it often enough.'

I had no choice, and minutes later I was packing my things. I was quiet during the bus journey to Stanhope Street, brooding. I'd miss St Patrick's. I'd liked the work there, but at least I wasn't being stuck back in that laundry, nothing could be as bad as that.

Arriving at the convent, we saw Sister Fidelis talking to a young woman at the gate.

'Ah! Here she is! Hello Kathleen. Hurry now, into this car. This poor woman hasn't all the time in the world. She's been waiting long enough for you.'

Wordlessly, I did what I'd been told. One sight of Sister Fidelis and I became a quivering wreck. The car drove off before I'd had a chance to say goodbye to my mother.

I looked out of the back window as we drove off, feeling great trepidation. Where were we going? And who was this pale, stick-thin woman sitting beside me? She must have been in her late twenties. She didn't smile, and wasn't bothering to talk to me either. My heart sank at what might lie ahead.

We travelled out of Dublin and through the countryside until we arrived in a street on the outskirts of a small town called Mulhuddart. Then the woman stepped out of the car, slammed the door behind her and headed for a box-like detached house. I climbed out too, and followed behind her. And it was the start of a very odd six months of my life.

My employer led me up upstairs to a tiny bare room. Then she took me downstairs to show me how to make coffee, squeeze juice and take care of the Aga. A tour of the characterless rooms followed. 'I expect you to keep the place spotless, Kathleen,' she said, and I nodded. Cleaning was second nature to me now.

I never got to know my strange employer, and I tried never to give her cause for complaint. If she hadn't treated me with such indifference I might have pitied her, because she led the loneliest life and her husband was rarely at home.

She was the daughter of the doctor at St Mary's, but I never learned her name, nor did I learn the address of the house. I don't remember letters being delivered; the phone never rang, nobody ever called and I was warned not to talk to any of the neighbours. Anyway, chance would be a fine thing since I wasn't allowed out, except to get fuel for the Aga.

I delivered a breakfast of freshly squeezed orange juice and coffee to my employer in bed each morning, but she never seemed to eat. The problem was it didn't occur to her that I might like more than just bread and butter, and I felt so guilty every time I ate that I felt unable to ask for more food. My weight plummeted to six stone.

I worked for that woman from 8.30 a.m. until 9 p.m. each day, when I would fall, exhausted, into bed. She made me work on the morning of my day off, and when I got back from seeing my mother the sink would be full of dirty crockery.

I don't know why I was scared of that woman, because in reality she was like a mouse. I suppose by then I was so used to doing whatever I was told that I didn't dare question her authority. So I went along with her when she allowed me just one bath a week, and I accepted that she didn't like me washing my clothes. She never once gave me clean sheets and I never asked for them, either. I did, once, ask her if I could borrow the iron, but she made such a fuss that I never dared to ask her again.

On a visit to my mother, I noticed in the newspaper that the Rotunda Hospital were looking for domestics, and it occurred to me for the first time that I didn't have to be beholden to those nuns, or to the jobs they supplied to me, for one minute longer. I was now 19. I'd had no life to speak of since the start of my teens. It was time for me to end the cycle of exploitation and show that I could think for myself.

Summoning up all my courage, I applied, using my mother's address, and was over the moon when they offered me a job in the paediatric unit at the rear of the hospital. When I told my employer that I was leaving she became angry.

'You can't do that,' she said. 'You've only been here for six months. The nuns said you'd stay a long time.'

I took a deep breath, and pulled myself up to my full height. 'I'm sorry they told you that,' I said. 'They had no right to.'

She blushed crimson. 'I'll tell them you're leaving,' she said, her pale eyes bulging with anger. 'They won't like it.'

I stood my ground, and felt that a heavy weight had been lifted from me. There really was nothing that the nuns could do to me. Not any more. And when she said, 'Is it the money? Because I can give you a raise from £1, to £1.50?' I felt like laughing in her face. And with my newfound confidence, I refused.

CHAPTER 10

KATHLEEN

I enjoyed my work in the Rotunda. It was much lighter than I had been used to. It was a case of mopping around the babies' cubicles and helping the nurses make up the babies' feeds. It was wonderful to be back in a hospital, even if I wasn't working as a nurse. I had my freedom and that was what mattered.

The boiler man would come into the kitchen sometimes, bringing his sandwiches with him. He would make himself a cup of tea and chat to us. One day, he took the milk from a big drum in the fridge and poured it into his tea. The nurse waited until he had taken a big sip, then she said, 'That's breast milk.'

I'll never forget the look of horror on his face. He spat his tea out and we all laughed.

At the Rotunda, life settled into a happy routine. We were fed well, so I gained weight, and I felt that I could leave the shadow of the laundries behind me. Sometimes a whole day would pass when I wouldn't even think about what I experienced there.

I was beginning to think I could leave those bad years behind when, in 1954, I developed a prolapsed womb. I was admitted to the gynaecology ward. The nurse told me to strip from the waist down and lie on the bed. There was a sheet hanging down to my waist, but she left my nether regions naked. I was horrified. Years of undressing under my nightgown, had left me extremely modest.

Noticing my discomfiture, she said, 'The doctors have seen it all before.' Then, rifling through my notes, she said, 'How many children have you got Kathleen?'

I looked at her, wondering if she was joking.

'Well?'

'I don't have any,' I said. She took another look at my notes, then shook her head, confused.

Just then a doctor swished back the curtains and swept in, bringing an entourage of young men behind him – I didn't know where to look. He fumbled between my legs, and stuck something up me. I gasped with shock and pain.

'Good girl,' he said, moving away, and I sighed with relief. Until he said, 'I'm just going to let my students have a look.'

And one by one, each of those young men prodded inside me. Having an internal examination is never nice. Having seven, six of them done by men with large hands and no skill, is excruciating. And remember, at 19 I was as green as grass. I didn't know the facts of life, and had had little or nothing to do with men. I fixed my eyes on a damp spot on the ceiling and tried to pretend that I wasn't really there.

The doctor talked to the students, asking them what they had found. 'Tell me,' he said, 'why does a woman have a prolapsed womb?'

'From childbirth.' This, from two of them in unison.

'Good answer,' he said. 'It usually happens when a woman has had a good few pregnancies. But this girl has had no children. Not one. So why do you think she ended up like this?'

'Could it happen from lifting heavy weights?' asked a gangly young man with glasses.

'It could.'

I tensed in shock. So all that back-breaking work I had done in the laundry had damaged me for life? It was quite possible, I realised, thinking of the strain I'd felt when we had hauled heavy sheets out of the big machines, ready for the calendar.

'We'll operate tomorrow,' said the doctor, writing in my chart, then he swept out and the six young men followed. One of them, the gangly one, smiled at me, and said, 'Are you okay?' I nodded, pleased at his kindness. But I wasn't. I was thinking about the laundry, and how the work there had led to this. *Had it marked me for life?* I started to cry.

Much as I liked my job in the Rotunda, I didn't see any future in it, or for myself in Ireland. I applied for a job with the Women's Royal Air Force – mainly because I liked the look of the blue uniform – and after an interview in Belfast I got the job.

After some initial training I set off for Oldenburg in Germany where I was to serve as a nurse. I adored it there, and my life opened up in a wonderful way. I loved my work, and I took up sport – representing the air force in table tennis, netball, hockey and running. It gave me status and got me noticed. And that was amazing to me, after a lifetime of being told I was good at nothing.

I made friends there too – and that included an RAF noncommissioned officer, who became my boyfriend. His name was Robbie, and we quickly became close. That, to me, felt miraculous – after all that I had been through. We went skiing to Winterberg in the Bavarian Alps, and as we skied down those stunning mountains, inhaling the crisp air, with the backdrop of snowy mountain peaks and the bluest blue sky, I felt as free as a bird – it was a million miles from the stultifying atmosphere of Stanhope Street.

By 1958, when I was a fully qualified nurse, the Luftwaffe were taking over the camp. Robbie was being sent to a secret bombsite at Eindhoven in Holland, while I got a two-year posting to Changi, the airbase in Singapore. I knew it was sunny and exotic there, but all I could think was how far away it would be from Robbie and how very much I would miss him.

He was silent when I gave him the news. But the next time we met he said, 'Marry me, Kathleen. And come to Holland with me.'

I agreed at once. It was strange. Marriage hadn't been on the cards for us before that moment, but suddenly it seemed like the only thing I wanted. Our friends were delighted for us, and we had a big celebration. When the Catholic padre heard about our engagement, he offered to marry us just as soon as we could get a wedding organised. I was all for it, but Robbie wasn't so sure.

'My parents would hate that. I'm an only child,' he said, then pausing, he took my hand, and looked me straight in the eye. 'Kathleen, would you mind if we got married in Britain?'

'No,' I said. 'No. That's fine.'

We were married in the Catholic Church in Clapham, London, with my mother in attendance, but it was done in a rush because we'd been called back to base. So I spent my honeymoon on a troop train then a troop ship. And when we arrived back, I had to stay in the WAAF block on my own as no married quarters were available. That was unbearable. We hated having to say goodnight and go our separate ways. I was moaning about this at work and one of the doctors said,

'There's a room in our house. You can have that if you like.'

'Oh, yes please,' I said.

'It's only small.'

And it was! There was just a Wentel bed – a single folding bed – and little room for anything else, but we didn't care. We were so glad of it, especially as it was in walking distance of the hospital.

In August 1958 I asked for my discharge from the WAAF, but this left me with no identification. I wrote to the Irish Embassy in Cologne asking for help in getting an Irish passport. To my great dismay, I was turned down. My own country – one that had treated me so badly, was now treating me like an alien. I was so upset, and I didn't know what to do.

Robbie suggested that instead I apply for a British passport, and so I became a British Citizen on 29 August 1958 at the British Consulate in Bremen. It wasn't quite what I wanted, but I was grateful.

After two years in Holland, we came back to Britain. We had a good marriage and were very happy – he was a rock to me, and had given me my future. I continued to nurse, and in due course two daughters came along, Tracy and Tina. I was worried that after my upbringing I would be unable to show them love, but to my relief it came naturally. We had the strongest of bonds.

We were looking forwards to Robbie's retirement and had bought a house in Bournemouth. After all those years of hard work, it was what he deserved. But in the early 1990s he became unwell, and was diagnosed with cancer. It was terrible watching him go through the chemotherapy. I felt helpless seeing him in such pain, and so wished I could help him through. When, in 1995, I watched him take his last breath, 38 years after we'd married, I was bereft. I was pleased, for him, that the long struggle was over, but life lost its meaning for me. I had lost my lifetime companion.

CHAPTER 11

KATHLEEN

After Robbie died, I thought about those days in the laundry more and more. I felt a burning need to share my secret with someone. It was on my mind every morning. Every single day I woke feeling I was back at Stanhope Street. At night, thoughts of the laundry looped through my mind. And the nightmares persisted.

I had never told Robbie about the laundry. I had pushed that time to the back of my mind. And besides I was ashamed. I thought he might think less of me if he knew. I was worried that he might end up leaving me.

That might sound far-fetched, and with Robbie's big heart was most unlikely, but I have met many Magdalene women since whose husbands can't cope with their wife's background. There are women who were orphans, or whose mothers were unmarried like mine, whose husbands call them a whore. They say, 'There must have been a reason for you being there.'

I had a good friend, Molly, who I had met through the church in England. We stayed in touch after she was widowed and moved back to Ireland. She was now living in Kilkenny. I felt that I could trust her so I wrote to her, and mentioned that I had been in a laundry. I didn't say much. I had to be terribly careful what I said because she was so strongly religious and I was concerned about how she would take it.

She was sympathetic, and I gradually increased what I told her. It helped to share my story after so many years. Each letter was hard to write, but it was cathartic too. It was as if writing the words freed me from the horror of the memories. Maybe, one day, I would be entirely free of them.

Molly rang one day sounding upset.

'Oh Kathleen,' she said, 'There was this programme on the telly last night. And I can't get it out of my mind.'

Haltingly, she told me the programme had been about four women who had been in Goldenbridge orphanage, run by the Sisters of Mercy. It had shown babies being beaten and scalded, and children treated with violence and cruelty. 'I can't believe it,' she said. 'That nuns should do such things.'

'That's terrible,' I said, thankful that I had never witnessed such behaviour at St Patrick's.

'And Kathleen. They used to strap the babies to potties and leave them there for hours sometimes.'

'But that's inhumane,' I said, then remembered, with a jolt, that I had done the same in St Patrick's. I'd had no choice, of course, but the memory made me ashamed, just the same.

The programme, *States of Fear*, has proved a landmark. I've since met Christina Buckley, the survivor of Goldenbridge who, in telling her story so bravely, opened the way for others to tell of their abuse. I cried when I learned she had died in 2014.

In 2002 Molly wrote to me saying she had heard about a Redress Board for everyone who had been in an institution.

This had been set up by the Oireachtas – the government – to administer a compensation scheme for anyone, including children, who were abused in an institution like an industrial school, reformatory or other institution since the formation of the state until the present.

She gave me an address and phone number, and the next morning I rang the number. But the girl who answered listened to me, and then said she would not send me the forms to fill in. She didn't say why, but it was obvious from her tone that she didn't believe me.

I was inconsolable when I put the phone down. And then I was plain furious. How dare that girl doubt my word? I made myself a cup of tea to calm myself down, then picked up the phone again. I said, 'You *must* send me the papers. I was in a laundry and I qualify.' She sighed, but said she would.

The papers arrived the following day. There were four centres listed to apply through. One of them was in London. I got in touch with them and that's how I met Phyllis Morgan. She came to see me, and listened intently as I spoke about my years in the laundry. I cried when I talked about Jane, the old woman who had died. I was embarrassed, but she just listened and handed me a tissue. Phyllis believed every word I said. Without question that felt indescribably good. After that first meeting we kept in touch and I am so grateful to her for the work she has done.

After meeting Phyllis I wrote to the Redress Board, in fact letters flew backwards and forwards over the next five years as I expanded on my years in the laundry. But they said Stanhope Street, where I had been, was not a laundry. They said it was a training centre for young women to prepare them for the world. I couldn't believe it. It was not a training centre. That was complete nonsense, a facade that had been painted for the public.

They didn't believe a word I was saying and turned down my application in 2004. But I wasn't going to let it rest. I appealed; more letters came but again, in 2007, after several misunderstandings about where St Mary's was and what address I lived at, my appeal was politely but firmly rejected.

I was so angry – for everything that I had been through. I deserved to be believed. I am not a liar and never have been. I phoned them again but was told, 'The case is closed. Your papers have been archived.' I had been in that terrible place for three long years, working for nothing, locked away from the world. What's more, that time in the laundry has affected my life ever since. And now I was being told that those three years never happened? This board had been set up to help people like me, and all they had done was hurt me.

After five years of correspondence, I could not accept that that was the end of the matter. I feared I would die without anyone ever knowing my story.

And then the phone rang.

'Hello, is that Kathleen Legg?' It was a male voice with a strong Cork accent.

'Yes,' I said, cautiously.

'This is Steven O'Riordan. I was wondering can I meet you?'

He said he'd heard about me through Phyllis Morgan. He was making a documentary about the Magdalene laundries. Phyllis was taking part in it, and had passed on my name. Would I like to be part of the film?

'Yes I will,' I said.

He laughed, sounding surprised. 'Don't you want to think about it?'

'No. I'll do it,' I said. I didn't hesitate. I hadn't been more sure of anything in my life. I thought, *If I'm filmed talking about my experience, and if people see me, they will know I'm telling the truth. And then, surely, the Redress Board will have to admit it too.*

He asked if he could come to Bournemouth to film me. We arranged to meet at the station, but when the train arrived I scanned the passengers, I couldn't see him. Then I felt a tap on the shoulder.

'Are you Kathleen Legg?'

I'd have recognised that voice anywhere. But I had mistaken this slight young man for a student. 'You're so young!' I said, unable to take my eyes off him.

'Well I'm 24,' he said, kissing me, and introducing me to two men carrying big silver camera boxes. I continued to stare at him, wondering how someone so young could deal with a dark subject like this one, and with women old enough to be his grandmother.

They piled into my Suzuki wagon and I drove them to a hotel for breakfast. As they tucked into bacon and eggs, Steven talked about the project, and my fears were put to rest. Steven was a very jokey type of person, but his kindness shone through, and he was clearly passionate about the need to tell the Magdalene story.

Breakfast finished, I drove them to my house, and they filmed me in my sitting room. It took a while to get used to the cameras, but soon I felt at ease. And it was good, telling him everything. He was shocked, yet I could see he believed every single thing I said. That felt wonderful.

I started to write my story out in an old copybook, and more memories would surface. I would post bits to Steven, piece by piece.

*

Steven continued filming, and the documentary, *The Forgotten Maggies*, was ready in 2009. He rang me one day, his voice trembling with excitement.

'I've great news,' he said. 'They're showing the documentary at the Galway Film Festival in July. Will you come over for the launch?'

'Yes,' I said. 'I'd like that.'

He appointed an American woman to act as my minder. She took me back to her apartment, and that evening we drove to Galway and had some tea in the hotel. There was a little girl there in an electric wheelchair. She had no arms or legs, but I was drawn to her lovely sweet smile. I said, 'Hello. Whose sister are you?'

'Steven's,' she said, and giggled. 'I want to sit with you.'

'Is that okay?' said a woman, standing, and picking the girl up in practised arms. 'This is Joanne and I'm her mother.'

I didn't know what to say to a 12 year old, but Joanne O' Riordan was so easy to chat to. She talked about school, and her friends, and I thought how remarkable she was. I'm not in the least surprised that she has gone on to achieve all she has – from shaming Enda Kenny's new government for reneging on its promises to the disabled to giving a speech to the UN.

Steven then beckoned me to go into a small room, and there I met the other women who were going to be featured in *The Forgotten Maggies*. Talking to them was both liberating and cathartic, because when I talked of the laundry they didn't react with disbelief or even with shock. None of them had been in St Mary's – many had been in laundries that sounded even worse – but we shared so many experiences in common. They too had worked on the calendar; they had lived in silence and had their self-esteem stripped away.

The next morning we met in the foyer but Steven seemed edgy. There was some problem with the documentary; it might not go ahead because of some technical issue. He said that a huge crowd had started to gather outside the cinemobile, a mobile theatre in the town centre of Galway. Hearing that, my legs began to shake with nerves.

The film festival organisers wanted to check the documentary before it was screened. Saying goodbye to us all, Steven headed off. For the next hour or so we sat in the foyer of the hotel. Then he rang Elaine, a local youth worker who had helped him from the start. She put her phone on speaker.

'It worked,' we heard him say. 'It looks unreal!'

'So they're showing it?' I had to be sure.

'Y-e-s, Kathleen. They're showing it.'

We left for the cinemobile two hours later, by taxi. When we saw the queue snaking down the street, our excitement grew.

I approached with the other women, and there were cameras all around us, going click, click, click, click; we linked arms and marched to the entrance. Steven met us and showed us to seats at the front. The theatre was full. As well as all the press, there were representatives from organisations like Barnardo's, Amnesty International and the Women's Labour Movement. Everyone's eyes were on us as we filed down the aisle.

This was to be the first time we had seen the film. I was shaking.

'If you find it upsetting, you don't have to stay,' whispered Steven. 'You can come out anytime you want.'

It was difficult to watch myself on screen, but even harder to see what other women had been through. Technicians carrying television cameras kept coming down the aisle, turning and facing us. I hated that.

'Don't let them see us cry,' I whispered to the woman beside me. I was determined to stay strong, but there was a part where they found the remains of some women in a convent's grounds, and I couldn't stop the tears from coming. I wasn't the only one. At the end we were directed to stand in front of the screen. And as the audience applauded us, I noticed most of them had tears in their eyes too.

That evening we were on the news. There I was, in my sober black trouser suit and pale pink jersey. It felt very strange.

Before I came home, Steven took me aside and asked me how I was and whether my family knew yet that I had been in a laundry. I said they didn't. I'd been putting off telling them.

'You must tell as soon as you get home,' said Steven. 'Imagine if they read it all in the papers first?'

I knew he was right. The next morning my face was all over the Irish papers. As I boarded the plane to return back to the UK, a woman approached me to say, 'Are you one of the ladies that was on the news last night?'

I said I was.

'Well done,' she said. 'Fair play to you.'

I was surprised that I was so instantly recognisable. As the plane took off, I started to worry about telling my daughters about the laundry. And as soon as I got home, I rang Tracy and Tina and said, 'I must see you. I've something to tell you.'

They came for tea the next day, and looked really worried. 'What is it?' asked Tracy.

'I haven't been in prison,' I said, seeing their anxious expressions. 'I haven't done anything wrong. But there is something I've been keeping from you.' I paused and took a deep breath. 'When I was a teenager, I was in a Magdalene laundry.'

'A what? You mean, like that movie?'

'*The Magdalene Sisters*?'

'Yes,' said Tina. 'That one with Anne-Marie Duff in it, and Geraldine McEwan as an evil nun.' She shuddered. 'That was *awful*!'

I nodded. 'It wasn't exactly like that. In some ways it was worse. Certainly there was mental cruelty.'

They stared at me, lost for words. Then I showed them the newspaper reports, showing a picture of us all at the Galway Film Festival. It was emotional. I cried as I told them more of my story, and they cried too.

'Did Daddy know?'

I shook my head. 'I couldn't tell him. I don't know why.'

Tracy put her arms round me. 'We'll support you,' she said. 'Any help you need, just ask.'

And they've been as good as their word.

I flew back to Ireland in September. There was to be a march in Carlow Town in support of all the survivors of the Magdalene laundries. On Sunday, 27 September 2009, we met outside a parish church. There was a huge banner saying 'Magdalene Women Marching for Justice', and hundreds of people turned out to support us, all of them wearing white ribbons as a symbol. Steven made a speech. He said an estimated 30,000 women were in the laundries.

'The physical, sexual, emotional and psychological damage these women suffered is unthinkable,' he said. And I felt pleased that, at last, all we had gone through was coming out into the open. We marched to the park and 13 doves were set free. They were to represent each of the Magdalene laundries. Then one of the women released a bunch of balloons.

I met Christine Buckley there, the wonderful woman who told her story back in 1999. *If she hadn't persuaded a film-maker to list the abuse she suffered in an industrial school in that programme,* States of Fear, *we would not be here today* I thought. When Christine died in 2014, there was a national outpouring of grief. The president himself attended her funeral.

I met another survivor too. Her name was Marina Gambold. She had come from Wexford for the march. She told me she had seen a screening of *The Forgotten Maggies* in Waterford, and it had brought back all her pain.

'It's so good to meet you Kathleen,' she said. 'All these years I hoped I would meet another woman from the Magdalene laundries, and I never did.' There were tears in her eyes.

In the evening there was a showing of *The Forgotten Maggies* in the ballroom of the Seven Oaks Hotel. There were hundreds and hundreds of people in the audience. After the showing, Steven asked us to stand at the front, as we had done in Galway. As we stood there, a man appeared with a cake covered in glowing candles. He held it out to me. I was baffled.

'I think you've got the wrong person,' I said. 'It's not my birthday.'

Hearing me, Steven, who had the microphone in his hand, said, 'We know it's not your birthday, Kathleen. We know your birthday is next month, but this cake is to celebrate all the birthdays you never had.'

The audience then sang a rousing version of 'Happy Birthday'. I stood there watching them, tears pouring down my cheeks unchecked. Tears, not for all those missed birthdays, but for this moment, when all my birthdays had come at once.

'Thank you,' I said. Then I blew out the candles.

CHAPTER 12

MARINA

ONE DAY, IN 2009, I was putting on the meat for the Sunday dinner when my neighbour, Kay, from across the road knocked on the door.

She said, 'Marina, there's something on in Dungarvan about the Magdalene laundries.'

'What's that?'

'They're showing a film.'

'Not that *Magdalene Sisters* one . . .'

'No no. A documentary.' Handing me the *Wexford People*, pointing to an advertisement, she said, 'Look. It's here. *The Forgotten Maggies*. I think we should go up and take a look.'

I was nervous, because I was once in one of those places and I didn't like to think about it. But I discussed the screening with my husband, Bill, after I had served up the chicken and roast potatoes, and he said, 'Of course you must go Marina.'

I was feeling fed up with the nuns back then, because I'd applied to the Redress Board set up for people who had been in an institution and had been turned down.

I didn't think many people would be interested in Magdalene laundries, but the cinema was packed tight. We sat, squashed into a row in the middle, and waited to watch the film. It showed women who had been in the laundries but who now lived in England. It really shocked me. I could not take my eyes off the screen. They were talking about things that had happened to them. Terrible things. And watching it I felt as if I was 17 years old again, and back in the Magdalene laundry in New Ross, County Wexford. I was shaking from head to toe.

'Are you alright, Marina?' asked Kay, seeing me dab at my eyes with a tissue.

'Yes,' I said. But then, seeing the look she gave me, I said, 'No. Not really.'

She squeezed my arm, and I noticed that she was crying too.

Not many people knew that I had been in a laundry. I didn't talk about it, not back then. But Kay was a good friend. I had known her for years. We talked about everything, and when one day I told her about New Ross, she had listened. And she didn't judge me.

At the end of the documentary, this young man stood up facing the audience. He had made the film, and he was in it, interviewing the women. He said he wanted to help women who had been in the laundries. He said there were thousands of women affected.

Kay nudged me. 'Did you hear that, Marina?"

'I did.'

'Thousands of women, he said.'

'Yes, I heard him.' My head was swimming with the realisation that I was not alone.

'Well?'

I looked at her. 'Well what?'

'What are you waiting for? Go and talk to him.'

By the time we got out of our seats and pushed our way along the row, the young man had gone. I was disappointed, realising I'd missed my moment. We made our way to the back of the cinema, carried along by the weight of the crowd, and soon we were out in the street. And there he was. He was surrounded by people, though, and I felt shy. 'He won't want to be bothered by the likes of me.'

Kay gave me a push, and propelled me towards him. I plucked at his arm. He turned round and I burst out, 'I was in a laundry. I was in one. I went through it too.'

I was sobbing. I couldn't stop. He looked a little alarmed, but he handed me his number and told me to ring him. And that's how I became involved in the Magdalene Survivors Together.

CHAPTER 13

MARINA

I WISH I had known my mother. I wish I knew what she was like. Everyone says she was like me, though I think she was taller. They say that before she got sick she was there for everyone in the street. She would do anything for anyone. That's like me. If she was alive today I would spoil her. I would. Poor, poor, Mary Kate.

When I was six, my mam was sick. She was dying, and my dad had already died. I would sit by her, and my two brothers Philip and Seamus would play at the end of the bed.

We spent a lot of time in my mam's room. We were frightened to let her out of our sight. We thought if we weren't there a doctor would come and take her away. He had visited, and had told her she must go to hospital, but Mam wanted to stay at home with us.

But one day an ambulance came. And a man Mam knew, called Mattie Kelly, got out of the ambulance and knocked at the door. 'We've come to take Mrs Mary Byrne to hospital,' he said.

'Why?' I asked.

'We hear she's very sick.'

He climbed the stairs, and Philip and I followed him. 'Mam they're taking you away,' I said, throwing my arms around her and hanging on tight, my tears soaking into her cardigan.

'She's right,' Mr Kelly said to Mam. He tried to lift her from the bed, but we were all hanging out of her, saying, 'No. Don't take Mam away.'

'Mary,' he said, 'the doctor is fierce worried about you. You know you're too sick to look after yourself, let alone all your children.'

'I'm not going,' said Mam, and she clutched onto the bed post. 'I'm not, and that's that. Not unless I can take my children with me.' She was crying, and I was crying, and little Seamus clung on to her and wouldn't let go.

But Mr Kelly insisted. He prised away our hands, put Mam on a stretcher, and off she went. And we never saw her again.

I was born in 1935, and we lived in a tiny cottage in Wexford Town. There was one bedroom, and we all slept in the same bed. That's just the way it was. We were poor, and we often went hungry. But the neighbours were good to us. They'd turn up with food. Without them I don't know what we would have done with my dad dead.

My mam had TB; my dad had died from that too. And there was a stigma in that. The kids in the area wouldn't play with us. I would go out sometimes with my skipping rope and a spinning top, and the other kids would run away, screaming.

'Agh . . . it's Marina Byrne,' they said, as they scarpered round the corner. 'Keep away!' Then they'd chant, 'The Byrnes have TB, the Byrnes have TB.'

That hurt so much. I knew it was something terrible bad, but

I didn't know what TB was. I don't expect they did either.

'What's TB?' I asked Philip, who I thought should know, being two years older than me. But he just shrugged.

There was a nun in the town called Sister Philip, and she was kind to us. She called to the house and gave us watery soup in an enamel mug and some dry bread.

The day that my mam went to hospital, an aunt from three streets away took us in. And soon afterwards, Philip and I were taken up to the county home. Little Seamus didn't come with us. He was only three years old, and he was taken in by another uncle and aunt.

It was terrible saying goodbye to him. He held onto me round my knees, and my aunt had to pull him off me. When we were driven away, I saw his little face at the window. And I could hear him, still screaming. I didn't see him again until he was 16.

Soon Philip moved on too. He disappeared one day. I didn't know it then, but he was taken to court by the cruelty man – which is what we all called the inspector of the Irish Society for the Prevention of Cruelty to Children – because he was destitute, and he was sent to Artane Industrial School. A lot of boys were sent there, back then. I missed him, and I missed Seamus. But I missed Mam most of all. I still miss her. I do. I cry whenever I think about her, and I think about her every day.

When we first arrived at the county home, we were stripped and washed from head to toe. The matron was kind. 'These poor children. Look at them!' she said. 'Look at all these boils. Look at these abscesses.' She lanced those, and all this pus came out. It hurt badly. 'Such neglect,' she said, and I got angry and cried out for Mam.

I have heard dreadful stories about the county home, but I was treated well. I don't know whether the matron felt sorry for me because I was always crying for my mam; or if it was because my mother's brother, James O'Rourke, worked there. But, whatever, I didn't stay there very long.

CHAPTER 14

MARINA

ONE DAY, WHEN I was just seven, Matron said, 'Marina, you're going to go and live with your grandmother.' She packed my few clothes, and she gave me a doll dressed like a Red Cross nurse, and it was the first doll I had ever had. I never had another one. I never had toys, or anything after that.

I was clutching the doll tight when I arrived at my granny's cottage in a small Wexford village called Raheen. I was excited to be going to Granny. I thought it would be like living with Mam again, but she seemed very, very old to me. She had white hair tied up in a bun and she was always cross. She was terrible posh. She had lived in America years before but she came home. I never knew my grandfather.

My granny used to say, 'I can't look at that child.' She would mutter it to herself, or to any visitors. 'She's so like her poor mother,' she'd say. I think she was still grieving for Mam, and missing her.

You'd think that would make her like me, but she'd murder me. She would get a sally switch and beat me with that, and I didn't know why. She would say, 'My Mary would still be alive if she hadn't married that sickly man.' She probably blamed us children for her daughter's death too.

My granny had wanted my mam to marry someone from the country because in those days, the Thirties, Forties and Fifties, townsmen didn't marry people from the country and country people didn't marry people from the town. My father was from the town and used to ride his bicycle out to my granny's house to meet my mother.

My granny was a great one for the church. She was very strict. She taught me my prayer book and my Bible, but filled me up with the fear of Christ. She taught me to work hard, and she always dressed me neatly. She was always saying, 'You will not show me up.'

When we went to Mass she would wear this fur stole. It smelt funny, all musty, and there was a fox's head on the end. The eyes used to look at me in church. I would kneel next to her, pretending to pray, and would peek through my hands, watching those eyes. Just in case the fox came alive and tried to take a bite out of me.

When I was nine years old Granny said, 'Marina, you're going to be confirmed.'

'But it's not time,' I said. 'That doesn't happen until sixth class.'

'I've asked specially,' she said. 'I asked the priest and your teacher, and they say they'll make an exception. '

But I didn't want them to make an exception. I wanted to be the same as the others. I was so much the youngest in that confirmation class. I knew all my prayers, and all the Bible stories, but I didn't like saying them in front of the older children or they'd taunt me. Mostly they just ignored me.

For the confirmation we had to go to the Sacred Heart

Church, Newbawn, some miles out of the village. I was dressed all smartly, but Granny said we were going in an ass and cart she had borrowed from a friend. I sat there getting bumped around, with Granny saying, 'Don't move Marina. Keep quite, quite still.' And I tried, hanging on for dear life, but it was so hard, especially when the cart swung around the corners.

My communion day wasn't happy. I was afraid – terrified of putting a foot wrong. As I lined up with the other girls and boys, waiting for my turn, I could feel my granny's eyes on me, waiting for me to make a mistake. I knew, if I did, she would knock me into the middle of next week. And though I did stumble over my words a little, I didn't forget anything.

I went to the national school in the village, and my best thing was spelling. I was very good at that, and at history too, but otherwise I wasn't great. At break time I ran around the playground with my friend, Kathleen. We would link one another and whisper secrets.

Sometimes this bigger girl with dark curls would call me names and knock into me on purpose. I was frightened of her, but Kathleen would stand up for me, and say, 'Leave her alone.' She was always on my side.

Our teacher, Tom Mahan, drove to school in a pony and trap. It took him a while, after school, to catch the pony and attach it to the trap. I'd be playing with Kathleen, and keeping an eye on Mr Mahan. When he started buckling all the straps I would race off home because Granny would be watching for him to pass by, and if he did, and I wasn't in the door, there would be all hell to pay.

'Where were you before now,' she would say. And out would come the sally switch.

My grandmother never, ever hugged me. God no! She never showed me any love, but that was normal in those days. I don't remember Mam putting her arms around me either, and I know she loved me. Everything was different then. Mothers didn't tell you that they loved you.

I hated it when my granny had visitors. As soon as the doorbell rang she'd shove me out into the yard.

'You're not to be listening and all, now,' she would say. And I would be out there, shivering if it was winter, waiting and waiting for the visitor to go home.

I spent a lot of time outside in the garden. From the time I arrived with my granny at seven years she had me working. I pulled up weeds in the garden, with two bags tied round my knees.

I dug and picked vegetables too, because Granny grew lots of food. I pulled up carrots, washed them, then ate them raw. I loved that. My granny worked hard, even when she was getting old. She wasn't rich, but we never went hungry. When I came home from school, there would be a bowl of potatoes or something roasted in the fire like bacon and cabbage. She baked bread and there were chickens as well, so there would always be eggs. At Christmas, my granny sold turkeys.

Santa never came at Christmas, and I never saw a Christmas tree. After Mass we would eat chicken, and we had rice pudding with coins in it. I didn't often have sweets. When my granny went for her pension, I used to pray that she would bring some home, but she never did.

At the end of the summer, we would be out picking blackberries all day, from early morning to late in the evening. We'd have them in a great big vat, then the man would come round. They were used for dye. Granny would sell them for two shillings, or half a crown.

She took me to work with her in a farmer's field too. We would take a can of tea and some slices of bread. She was a tough one, even in her eighties. I didn't love her, but my granny taught me respect. And, though I didn't know it then, showing respect would help me survive all that was to come. And, more important, I think my granny made me a nice, kind person.

CHAPTER 15

MARINA

WHEN MY GRANNY was 89, and I was 15, she slowed down a little. She stopped going out to work and left the garden and tending the vegetables entirely to me. Then she took to the bed. I'd hear her coughing and spluttering, and she wouldn't eat. The doctor came, and coming down the stairs, he looked grave.

'Your granny must go to hospital,' he said, and later that day the ambulance came to collect her. That was a terrible shock to me. Watching her go, I wondered if I'd ever see her again. Or would it be a repeat of that awful day when my mam was carted off, away from us. I was confused that day, and wondered what would happen to me now. I couldn't stay alone in my granny's house. But that evening, a middle-aged woman appeared on the doorstep, her brown hair pulled severely into a bun.

'I'm your Aunt Lily,' she said. 'You're coming home with me.'

I gathered my scant belongings, and we took the bus to her house in Enniscorthy. I thought it would be nice, living with her and my Uncle Thomas, because they had nine children, including some girls around my own age. But I was wrong.

The two fair-haired girls lying on the bed looked at me, when Aunt Lily showed me up to the tiny bedroom I was to share with them and their younger sister, but they didn't seem very friendly. Aunt Lily beckoned me downstairs without introducing them, and set me to washing some dishes.

When Uncle Thomas returned from his work at St Senan's, the 'mental hospital', he shook my hand and smiled. He had twinkly eyes and I instinctively liked him. 'I miss your mother,' he said. 'She was a lovely woman. And Marina, you're starting to look a great deal like her.'

I smiled with pleasure but Aunt Lily scowled, as if she didn't want to be associated with anyone who had died from TB.

In the morning my cousins went off to school. I'd have liked to go with them, but I'd finished school by then, so I stayed behind and slaved for Aunt Lily. She had me doing all the washing and all the dusting, sweeping and scrubbing too. It was hard, picking up after my cousins. The girls, Eileen, Stella and Elizabeth, treated me with indifference. Their mother encouraged that. 'You're just a poor orphan,' they said, glancing up from their studies.

It was hard to sleep. I'd wake every time one of the girls turned over or sighed in their sleep. I'd lie there, thinking of Granny, wondering if I could soon go back to her. I asked Aunt Lily if I could see her, and she took me to the community hospital in New Ross.

Walking into this huge ward, with beds lined down the side, I couldn't see Granny anywhere. Aunt Lily led me to this very old lady who was lying there, her white hair loose, straggling around her face, and I realised with a shock it was Granny. Her mouth seemed sucked in. There was a terrible rasping noise coming from her throat. I was scared she would stop breathing while we were there. A few days later, as I was chopping cabbage, Aunt Lily told me she had died. I was sad, but I didn't cry.

I was with my uncle and aunt for 18 months, but my aunt's attitude never softened towards me. I think she only let me live there because it made her look charitable. Once I heard Mrs Doyle from next door say, 'Lily, you are such a good Christian. Nine children already, and look how good you have been to Marina!'

Aunt Lily loved that. She smiled smugly, and said, 'Well, I do what I can.'

And I thought of all the work I did for her, without payment or much thanks. When I was almost 17 my aunt said one day, 'Pack your things Marina, I'm taking you into the convent in New Ross.'

'The convent?'

'That's right. The Good Shepherd's. I've been talking to Father Ryan from the mission up in Enniscorthy. He spoke to the nuns, and they will be happy to have you. He says it's a great place for young girls.'

I was wild excited. My granny had died, nobody wanted me, and I was going to learn new things. That would be better than slaving here for my aunt! I was thinking how kind she was to let me go, and I wondered who would do the housework now. I skipped around the room while I gathered all my belongings. Not that I had much.

'Hurry up Marina,' she said. 'Or we'll miss the bus.'

The bus? We were going on a bus? I smiled to myself. I had enjoyed the only other bus journey I'd taken in my life – on the way to my aunt from Granny's house.

*

We walked from the bus stop up to this dreary grey building. There were steps up to a massive carved oak door. My aunt rang the bell and I heard it echoing inside but, for a while, no one appeared. Then the door creaked open and there stood this tall nun, wearing thick-lensed glasses. I looked down, not wanting to meet her eye, and noticed the shine on her lace-up shoes.

My aunt pushed me forwards. 'This,' she said, 'is Marina.'

CHAPTER 16

MARINA

'MARINA? AH YES,' said the nun, and took my little bag from me. 'You're the new orphan, aren't you? I've been expecting you. I'm Mother Scholastic, and from now on *your* name is Fidelma.'

I hated the name Fidelma. But I didn't dare say so. I had been taught to show respect, and I was scared of that nun. I couldn't think why they would want to change my name at all, but later found out they gave everyone new names. I suppose it felt normal to them, since every nun took on a new identity when they joined the convent.

My aunt reminded Mother Scholastic of why I was here. That my grandmother had died and there was nobody to care for me.

'I've done my duty by her,' she said. 'She's been with me for a while now, but I haven't the time to guide her, with my big family to care for. And the parents. Well they died some years ago. From TB.' She whispered this last bit, as if it was a disgrace to die that way.

Nodding brusquely, the nun turned to me. 'Now Fidelma, listen to me. You are never to tell anyone here your old name. Do you understand?'

I nodded, miserably.

'And you are not to tell them why you are here.'

Well that suited me fine. I didn't want the world to know my parents had been poor, and had caught TB. That was nobody's business but mine.

Mother Scholastic led me down a long corridor with a tiled floor and up some stairs to the top of the building, to a room lined with shelves of clothes. She handed me a navy dress, thick stockings and some battered shoes. 'Put these on, and hurry,' she said. Then, as I struggled with the laces, she took my own dress and shoes from me. I never saw them again until the day I left that place, and that's the truth.

'Fidelma, you know why you're here, don't you?'

'Yes Sister.'

Before I could continue, and say it was to prepare me for the world, she said, 'You're here to do penance for your sins. And you will be working every day in the laundry.'

I wondered what my sin was. I hadn't done anything wrong, had I? I was just orphaned, but I didn't ask. She showed me up to a high-ceilinged room packed full with iron beds. She led me over to a bed in the middle. Pointing to it, she said, 'This is where you'll be sleeping.' Putting my bag down, I noticed how thin the mattress was. It was lumpy too. I wondered if I would be sharing it and, if so, with how many?

A bell rang and Mother Scholastic said, 'It's time for tea.' We went downstairs again, and all these girls and women were standing in a line. Mother Scholastic pushed me behind them, and one of them turned round and looked at me, but she didn't say 'Hello'. I smiled at her, but she just turned back and faced the front. *That's not very friendly*, I thought.

Another bell rang and we walked into a cavernous room with long tables, and, following the girl in front of me, I stood at one. Then a nun, who was looking down on us from a kind of throne, said grace, and we all sat down.

I was hungry, and was surprised when just a plate of dry bread came round, and then a saucer of dripping. Was this all we were to get? I wanted to ask the girl beside me, but nobody was talking so I didn't dare. We were each given a small cup of tea. I watched the other girls put the saucer on top of the cup, and I wondered why. Then I noticed that the dripping melted, and they dipped the bread into it. I did the same, devouring my measly meal, but the hunger was terrible.

I was hungry after tea, when we went to a big room to sew for the nuns, and I was hungry when we queued by the stairs waiting to go to the dormitory for bed. My stomach ached with emptiness when I lay in my own bed, listening to all the girls breathing and snoring in theirs. And I cried. I cried for Philip, for Seamus, and for my mam. And I cried for myself. Because with my granny dead, there was nobody in the world who wanted me.

A bell woke me very early in the morning. I followed the girls down to church for Mass. While we prayed, I opened my eyes, and looked around at the Holy Statutes. I loved the one of our Lady. I hoped she was watching over me.

By the time we queued for breakfast, I was dizzy with hunger. I hoped there would be porridge, or maybe an egg, but it was bread and dripping again. It always was, every day.

After breakfast we were put to scrubbing floors, and polishing all the corridors. I had to scrub all the cloisters on my hands and knees. It was so hard and my knees ached afterwards. Over the months they became more painful and started to swell up. I told Mother Scholastic, but she said pain was part of my penance.

After the cleaning had been inspected we were put to the laundry for the rest of the day. My first day I was shown around by Sister Leo.

'This is a very important job we do here Fidelma,' she said, her double chin wobbling.

And I whispered to myself, 'My name is Marina.' Would I ever get used to being Fidelma?

'There's all this laundry here,' she said, pointing to bags and bags that had arrived that morning. 'It comes from all round the county of Wexford, and from County Carlow too.' She puffed out her chest with pride.

She led me into a room filled with steam. There were rows of girls working on enormous metal machines, feeding in sheets. 'This is the calendar room,' she said. Next she showed me the washroom, full of a whining noise, as these giant machines spun around. Some young girls were washing clothes by hand, some of them were so small that they had to stand on a box so that they could reach the sinks and swirl the clothes around with a stick. Two bigger girls were scrubbing a carpet with brushes with a long handle. They were red faced with exertion. It looked like terrible hard work, and I turned and walked out of the room, before Sister Leo had a chance to ask me to join them there.

'This is the mattress room,' she said, showing me girls who were teasing out old mattresses, covering them with new ticking to make them good – nobody bought a new mattress back then. Other girls worked in the sewing room, on the fancy smocking used mostly for children's dresses. I watched one girl with round glasses hard at work weaving her needle through the fabric, and thought, *That is beautiful!* I'd never worn anything so beautiful in my younger life. I was just thinking, *I hope I get picked for this*, when Sister Leo bellowed at her.

'You!' she said, and snatched the little dress the girl was working on. 'You think we will be able to sell *this* in Harrods?' She threw it back at her. 'You do know it's the poshest shop in London? Take it out and start again. Every mistake costs money. And don't you *ever* forget it.'

The girl looked as if she was about to cry, and the others in the room, keeping their eyes on their work, started to tremble with fear. I thought, *I don't want to work here after all.* I knew I wouldn't be able to do such fancy work.

Looking me up and down as if I was cattle, Sister Leo said, 'I think we'll put you on the presses. You're a good strong girl, that will suit you.'

Leading me in to the pressing room, she handed me a white coat – the sort doctors wear, and showed me another that had already been pressed. I looked at the machine, a menacing looking contraption which was hissing steam. I trembled, wondering how I would manage the work without burning myself to death.

My first two attempts at pressing the coats weren't good. 'You've pressed in some creases, you careless girl,' shouted Sister Leo, throwing the coat on the ground. 'Try another.'

It was hard when I was trembling, and had her bready eyes watching every move, but the next one was better, and I soon learned how to do it. It was monotonous work, and tiring too. But after a few days, I felt as if I had been doing it for my entire life. I sighed remembering how, once, I'd thought pulling out vegetables in my granny's garden was hard work. *What I wouldn't give, right now, to swap this steamy room for that wonderful fresh air.*

*

We finished at the laundry in the late afternoon. I'm not sure what time, because time meant nothing to us. It was just bells. In the evenings we would sit in circles in a great big room sewing for the nuns. I was responsible for devotional scapulas – an item made by putting holy images or text onto pieces of cloth, which we then joined together with bands of material for people to wear over their shoulders. I made holy pictures too, which the nuns would sell. There would be a big sale for the public every year, and everything was snapped up. But we were kept away from that. And we certainly didn't see any of the money. Those nuns made money out of us every way they could, and they never gave us a penny. Not one.

When I worked in the laundry I had my sewing with me all the time. When we walked to lunch, or when we asked permission to go to the toilet, you would take it out and sew as you walked along. Your head would be down, concentrating. One day I needed the toilet in a hurry, and I didn't take the scapula with me. Mother Scholastic saw me and screamed out, 'You! Where is your sewing? The devil finds mischief for idle hands.' She said that all the time.

When it was time for bed Mother Scholastic would stand at the bottom of the stairs with her arms folded. She would shout out our names and we would line up in order. Then it was up to bed, undress, wash and say prayers. And it was the same old routine day after day.

CHAPTER 17

MARINA

I HAD HOPED to make friends in the laundry. There were a lot of girls who looked the same age as me, but we were in silence for most of the day. I found that terribly hard. If we were caught even whispering they'd be at us, roaring, or in the worst cases doling out a beating or a punishment – like extra work, or standing for hours in the corridor outside the dormitory.

That's not to say that we worked in silence. There was always the roar of the boilers and the hiss of steam from the presses. If I shut my eyes I can still hear that racket, even after all these years.

Nothing got past Sister Leo. She would be sitting in the laundry, or in the dining room, on her throne, her eagle eyes trained on us. She would notice if our lips moved, and would report us at once. It was so hard.

I waited and waited for lessons to start. I thought, if I am being prepared for the world, I will need to be taught how, but after some weeks had passed I realised my turn in the classroom would never come.

I missed reading and writing. There were no books in the place, except for the prayer books and Bibles, and we had no paper or pens. That meant we couldn't pass notes as a way of talking. What were they trying to do to us? I wondered if this was all part of my penance. And if it was, how long would it take before I was absolved of whatever sin they believed I had committed?

There were younger children living in an orphanage on the other side of a long tunnel, near the nun's quarters. We could see them playing, sometimes, across the yard. We never met them, but hearing their cheerful laughter, I envied them. Or I did, until I realised that when they were 16 they would most likely end up in the laundry with me; me and the other 79 others who lived with me in that hell hole.

I couldn't imagine how the older women in the laundry felt. They had been there, living in silence, for most of their lives. Had they forgotten what life was like outside? But most Magdalene women were young like me – from 16 years upwards. I think a lot of the girls had come from the county home, and quite a few had had a child.

They weren't allowed to tell us that, but we always knew who they were because there was a sadness about those girls. I'd hear them crying out in the dormitories, and whenever the nuns scolded them it was always 'you prostitute'. I didn't know what a prostitute was – but I knew it was bad. It was worse, even, than being an orphan.

After a few weeks the routine seemed less confusing. I was like the others now, knowing where to go when each bell rang, acting like a robot, walking with my head bowed.

I had been promoted at work. I was still in the pressing room, but now I was doing all the pleating on skirts and anything else that needed pleating. This was more skilled work and I was good at it, taking a pride in making the clothes perfect. Sister Leo would try and find something wrong, but when her assistant, Sister Bernard came to inspect my work, she said, 'But this is perfect Fidelma. You're a great girl, so you are,' and I smiled, feeling pleased. It was a small act of kindness, but meant so much to me in that horrible harsh environment. I thought of my granny, and how proud she would be that I was doing my work so well. Because it was she who had taught me to give only my best.

I liked Sister Bernard. She was the only nun who was nice to me, ever. She was young and lovely, with a fresh complexion and lively eyes. I admired her.

A few months after I had arrived at the laundry, it was the Reverend Mother's Feast Day and that meant a big celebration. There was great excitement about it, and I couldn't think why. It was true we would be let off work, but all it meant to me was more prayers. Then a girl whispered, 'We get an egg today,' and my mouth began to water in anticipation.

I thought about my egg all the way through Mass, waiting for breakfast with such longing. And sure enough, the dish holding them all came round. There was one for each of us. I had never forgotten the eggs from my granny's house; I collected them straight from the hens, with feathers still attached, and watched while she boiled them over the fire.

I loved the runny yolk, and the firm white. I smiled to myself, as this one precious egg was handed to me, thinking how I would dip my bread into the yolk. I cracked it open, but there was no liquid yolk. It was like a blooming bullet. I nearly cried with disappointment. So when, on Easter Day, we were told we would be having an egg for breakfast again, I just sighed. And, sure enough, it was as hard as a bullet again.

CHAPTER 18

MARINA

ONE DAY, WHEN I'd been in the laundry for a month or so, Sister Leo came into the pressing room and told me I had a visitor.

'It's your aunt come to see you,' she said. 'Go and brush your hair and spruce yourself up.' I did, before following her through this tunnel to the parlour. The tunnel was dusty and dimly lit – with pipes running across the ceiling. Something landed on my face, and I screamed. Sister Leo slapped me hard, on the side of my head. 'Don't be a baby,' she said. 'It's just a spider, fallen down from a web.'

I walked into the parlour, and there was Aunt Lily sitting in a chair, ramrod straight. Mother Scholastic sat opposite her; she pointed to a third chair, telling me to sit. I looked from one of them to the other, wondering if I was in trouble, or if Aunt Lily wanted me back to slave for her in the house. If she did, I knew I'd go with her like a shot – and yet I didn't want to admit that living with her was preferable to being here. As it turned out, I wasn't asked to comment.

It was Mother Scholastic who did the talking.

'Fidelma is very happy here,' she said. 'She's settled well, isn't that right Fidelma?'

'Yes Mother,' I said. It wasn't true, far from it, but I knew if I said any different I'd be in for a punishment.

'You're a lucky girl Marina; I mean Fidelma,' said Aunt Lily, taking off her gloves and holding them carefully in her left hand. 'And don't you forget it!'

'You can rely on us to prepare Fidelma for the world,' said Mother Scholastic.

'I don't doubt it.' Aunt Lily went on and on, saying the nuns were great people altogether. And how she knew they would teach me well. 'You will learn everything you need to know here,' she said.

I just nodded. I wasn't at all happy, but I didn't say anything to her. There would be no point. I suspect she'd only visited because she felt the nuns would expect it. She came once more, then I never saw her again, but I wasn't too sorry. She was one of those ones, always in with the nuns and the priests, but she was an old divil. She never even brought me anything. But then I didn't expect it, not from her.

The weeks dragged into months and it was as if I had never experienced a different life. There was nothing to look forward to – it was just a monotonous diet of bread, dripping hard labour and loneliness. And the longer I was in there, the lonelier I became.

That sounds mad when I was never, ever, entirely alone, not even for a minute. But when you can't talk, when you can't ask 'where are you from, and what are you doing here?', you can be more lonely than you would if you never saw another soul.

We lived with desperate fear. Fear of the nuns, and fear of punishments. And we had good reason to be. One night Sister

Leo dragged in a girl who'd just arrived. 'Everyone, look at Evelyn,' she said. 'We found her trying to escape.'

The girl was sobbing. 'I just wanted to see my baby,' she said.

Slapping her hard across the face, Sister Leo screamed, 'Forget your baby and do your penance.' Spit flew out of her mouth and sprayed across Evelyn's pale cheeks. Sister Leo's face was red with anger, and her chins wobbled more than ever. She commanded one of the older women to bring her some scissors. Roughly yanking hold of Evelyn's fine, fair curls, she hacked away at them with the blunt scissors. Evelyn streamed tears as her beautiful long blonde hair fell to the floor in a heap. My heart bled for her, but there was nothing any of us could do. Evelyn looked a terrible fright afterwards, and she cried noisily as she picked the long strands off the floor, as ordered, and threw the hair away. 'Look at her,' said Sister Leo again. 'This is what will happen to you all if you all if you try and escape.' I didn't need to be told.

I was desperate to get outside those high walls but I couldn't see how it could be done. There was broken glass cemented in, so that anyone trying to climb out would be cut to ribbons, and there was barbed wire on the top of the wall.

Besides, if I did manage to escape, where would I go and what would I do? Nobody wanted me. The nuns told me I was less than nothing. However hard I worked for them, whatever I did for them, Mother Scholastic and Sister Leo never once showed me or any of the others the slightest bit of respect. Never. It was only abuse. The longer I stayed there, the more I felt the nuns were right. Maybe I *was* less than nothing, and maybe being an orphan *was* a sin.

CHAPTER 19

MARINA

ONE MORNING AT breakfast there was fierce excitement. 'Today is a very special one,' said Mother Scholastic. 'The new Queen in England is being crowned. We've got a wireless, and you may listen.'

We never normally knew what was going on outside the convent walls. Apart from the nuns, the only people we ever saw were the men who came in the van to pick up the laundry. And they never talked to us. They couldn't with Sister Leo or Mother Scholastic standing there, glaring at the girls who took in the dirty laundry or gave out the clean.

So it was exciting getting this chance to witness such a wonderful ceremony. We all looked at each other and smiled. We formed a circle round the radio and listened, entranced. Although there were only words, I could see Queen Elizabeth in my mind. And I wished and wished I was one of the crowd waiting outside Westminster Abbey or Buckingham Palace to wave to the new Queen of England.

From that day on I dreamed of going to England. I used

to pray about it to the Blessed Virgin Mary. I just wanted to get out of Ireland because it was such misery. In Ireland I was always hungry. In Ireland I was an orphan. In Ireland I was a sinner.

It was while daydreaming of England that I burnt my hand very badly. By then I was used to hearing, 'that will soon heal', so I knew that no treatment would be given. My fingers were covered in scars from blisters that had burst.

One day, though, pressing a skirt, I slipped and fell. I put out my arm to stop myself, but it landed against the press, scalding the whole of my lower arm. I screamed in agony, smelling the burning skin, and as the day went on I watched as the blister spread leaving my arm red raw. By the time we queued for bed I was crying in pain. I couldn't help it – my arm was a burning, blistering lump of charred meat.

Hearing my sobs, Mother Scholastic grabbed me by my burned arm and I screamed out in agony. She didn't care. She barely glanced at my arm.

'Stop that nonsense,' she said and shook me hard. 'Just stop it, or I'll give you something to cry for.' I tried to stop, but my arm was just so sore.

It hurt for days and days, and the dye from my dress worked its way into the wound, making it worse. But I didn't dare complain, and I cried silently, because the nuns seemed to like to see us in pain. It was part of our penance. They were very hard and spiteful.

There was a lot of praying in the laundry. There was Mass in the morning, and prayers in the evening. And we had to be there, always. In May we had to walk around the grounds every day as well, praying and praying. I don't know what good our prayers did.

One day I broke a cup at breakfast time. Drinking tea, I put my cup too close to the edge of the table and when I put the saucer of dripping on top of it, it toppled over and smashed onto the floor. The crash reverberated round the refectory, and everyone turned round and watched as the slivers of china shot in all directions. The tea made a terrible big puddle. My face burned with embarrassment. I held my breath, my heart sinking, wondering what would happen next.

'Go and fetch the mop and clear up that mess!' screamed Sister Leo, towering over me. 'Now pick up every piece of china – the splinters too.' When I had finished, and Sister Leo had checked to see that I had done it properly, she fetched some rope, looped it round the handle of the cup, and made me wear it round my neck. I felt so stupid. And she made me wear that cup round my neck for three days and three nights.

Everyone stared at me, and at night when I turned over in bed the jagged edge poked into me, waking me. I didn't dare take it off. But that wasn't the only punishment.

For the next three days there was no chair for me at the table in the refectory. I had to eat my food off the floor like a dog. Everyone stared at me, but the worst thing was my sore knees. I nearly cried with the pain of them.

After three days, which was nine meals, I was made to kneel in front of Mother Scholastic. I had to say, 'I beg almighty God's pardon, our Lady's pardon, Mother Scholastic's pardon and my companions' pardon for the bad example I have shown.' I will never forget those words.

After I had spoken them, Mother Scholastic went on looking at me.

'Have you forgotten something Fidelma?' she said.

I looked at her in puzzlement, not sure what she expected. Then I noticed a girl sitting at another table bow her head very slightly. And I remembered. I bowed my head, very low, and said, 'Please Mother. Can I have my chair back?'

She nodded. 'You have done your penance Fidelma. But let that be a lesson to you.'

CHAPTER 20

MARINA

WE HAD NOTHING to look forward to in the laundry. We didn't have birthdays, and we didn't celebrate Christmas either. Not really. We'd get a bag each with Palmolive soap and shampoo for our hair. It was nice to wash our hair with shampoo and not carbolic soap like normal, but that was our only payment for doing an adult's job. And the shampoo never lasted until the next Christmas, no matter how hard we tried to ration it.

Mother Scholastic was our boss. She was always saying, 'Be careful now, or I will send you to Roscrea.'

I didn't know Roscrea from Adam; I don't think any of us girls did, but her words would make us shake. Because if Mother Scholastic thought going there was a punishment, then it must really be worse than New Ross. And we couldn't even imagine anywhere worse.

The nuns were very hard and they were spiteful too. We knew we would be punished if we talked, but sometimes we were punished for things we didn't know were wrong. One night, finishing up work for the day, we noticed there was a beautiful full moon. Three of us ran onto the veranda to have a better look. It was so bright and beautiful – and lord knows it had been a long time since I'd seen a thing of beauty.

Starting to shiver, we turned to go back in, when the door slammed behind us. We heard the lock clicking and saw a nun watching us through the window in the door. It was freezing cold out there, and we only had our uniform dresses on. Our slippers, made from the off-cuts of the mattresses tied with string, did little to stop the damp cold seeping in. We banged on the door, but the nun just looked at us stony faced. 'You shouldn't have been out there, so you shouldn't. And you should certainly not be out wearing those slippers. I'm leaving you there to teach you a lesson.'

We huddled together trying to get warm, but we couldn't. We blew on our hands, and rubbed them together, anything to make them warmer. We waited and waited for someone to come and let us in again, but we were left out there all night. It was midwinter, and it felt cold enough to snow. We lost all feeling in our hands, in our noses, in our feet. We sang, softly, trying to keep our spirits up, but I have never felt so cold in my whole life. We nearly froze to death.

I've never forgotten how that felt. I think of it on cold mornings, even today. We have a conservatory in our house in Wexford and, when I walk in there to water the plants on frosty mornings, the cold damp gets into my bones and brings that night back with real resonance.

The next day, when the nun finally unlocked the door, we ran in, our lips blue with cold. She didn't ask us how we were, or suggest we have a cup of tea in order to warm up a little. She just said, 'Hurry down to Mass now.' My fingers and toes were so cold I thought I'd never feel them again.

After breakfast it was cleaning as usual, and then to the laundry. My head was spinning so much, it took all my concentration to work that press. It was hard to work; hard to concentrate; hard even to think. I burnt myself on the presses, my fingers still numb. But it wasn't too bad a burn, so I didn't tell anyone as there was no point. I got used to living with a bit of pain. My chest felt tight, and by the end of the day I had a hacking cough. I felt sick for days. I will never, ever forget that. And I will never forgive those nuns for it either.

The nuns were bad to me, but they were worse to the girls who came from the county home in Enniscorthy. They had nobody in the world. Most of them had had babies that were fostered or given for adoption, and their families wouldn't have them home again. They had disgraced them.

One day a girl arrived from England. A priest had brought her to the convent. She was screaming and crying, and the nuns gave her a terrible time. She was beautiful, with long gingery hair. The nuns called her a prostitute.

'You have a lot of sins to atone for,' she was told. She was desperate to get out of the laundry. She had run away from home and had been living with her boyfriend in England. Her family never wanted to see her again. She was a disgrace to them.

Every night I would hear her moaning and crying. She was always in trouble, because she was crying too much to work properly. One day she just wasn't there anymore. I don't know where she went. Maybe she ran away; or maybe she was sent to Roscrea. I would love to have known, but you couldn't ask.

The nuns called us all fallen women. But the only time I fell was when I fainted with hunger. I didn't know anything about men. I had never been with a man. Sometimes I wish to Christ

I had had a baby like those other girls as then he or she might come looking for me now. But I never had one. I have only got my husband.

Some of the girls were sent to jobs away from the laundry. They wanted to go and would work on farms, or with people the nuns knew. I was terrified of being sent, because usually the girls came back again in a worse state than before. They were treated badly. Some became pregnant and had a baby before being sent back to the laundry. I was terrified that would happen to me.

Many girls had visitors. After my aunt's two visits I had no one. Other girls were the same. Many of them had been put in the laundry by the state. The state had responsibility for us, but they never checked up on us. And if no one came to see you, it was like you belonged to the nuns and they could do whatever they liked with you. You had nobody. Nobody in the world to give you a bit of encouragement and love.

CHAPTER 21

MARINA

ONE DAY, WHEN I was 19, Mother Scholastic sent for me. I walked down the tunnel and into the parlour to find my Uncle John sitting there. I liked Uncle John. He was Mammy's brother, and had helped us when Mammy was dying. I had seen him now and then when I'd been living with Aunt Lily, and he was always kind to me. There was a young man sitting beside him. I hadn't a clue who *he* was.

'Marina?' the young man said. 'Is that you?'

'Well I'm Fidelma now,' I said, wondering who the slight built man was.

'Marina, I'm Philip. Philip, your brother.'

I looked at him in confusion, trying to see the little boy I had once known.

'Marina, I've been searching for you for years,' he said. 'But what's happened to you? You're skin and bone?' He was crying, and I felt like crying too. But Mother Scholastic was staring at me, and before I could answer, she cut in.

'Fidelma is a good worker and she's happy here,' she said.

'And besides, she can't leave here; she's not ready to go.'

'I don't care, I'm taking her,' said Philip, his voice strong and proud.

'You can't.' Mother Scholastic drew herself up to her full height. 'There are procedures. We're caring for Fidelma for the state.'

Philip looked at her in fury. I thought, for a minute he would hit her, but Uncle John put a hand on his arm and said, 'Steady now Philip. Anger won't do any good.'

I stared at the floor, not knowing what to think. I wanted to contradict Mother Scholastic, and to tell Philip how much I had missed him, but I was too scared to open my mouth. If I contradicted Mother Scholastic she'd have it in for me later.

Smiling in triumph, Mother Scholastic sent them away. My uncle rose from his chair, then beckoned to Philip indicating he should get up too. But Philip was staring at me, in a trance, and it wasn't until my uncle had taken his hand and pulled him up that he came out of his reverie. Then with one last look at me he allowed my uncle to usher him away.

I cried when they had gone. I didn't know what to think. I wanted to leave the laundry so much, in one way, but I was terrified too. I lay in bed that night, thinking about Philip, wondering how life would have been if Mam and Daddy hadn't died.

Three weeks my later my uncle and Philip came back, and this time they were insistent that I go with them. I was very happy when Mother Scholastic told me, which is more than I can say for her. She glared at me as I went off to gather up my few belongings before leaving with my long lost brother. I didn't have a chance to say goodbye to the other girls in the laundry; they were at work, and I've regretted that since. But the nuns never liked penitents to see other girls leaving. I think they felt it would unsettle everyone, and they liked there to be an air of mystery about where someone had gone.

As I walked through that door I was shaking with nerves. In the laundry I had been safe. Would I survive outside the high walls, or were the nuns right when they said I wasn't yet ready to go? I carried with me my small bag containing the few rags I'd arrived in. The nuns didn't give me a penny. Not one penny for all the work I had done all those years. There was never a mention of payment. Not from the day I went in to the day I went out.

I was quiet as the bus made its way near my uncle's house. I sat beside Philip, staring blankly out of the window, wondering what had happened in the years since I'd been incarcerated. I wondered how Uncle John had become involved in my plight, but those questions could wait. First I wanted to know Philip's story.

When we got to my uncle's house, we sat down with a cup of tea – and Philip began to tell me.

'I was in Artane Industrial School,' he said.

I hadn't heard of it, not then. 'And is it nice?' I asked.

He and my uncle exchanged a glance and I said, 'What? What is it, Philip?'

'Show her your hands, Philip,' my uncle said. And slowly Philip held them up for me to see. His fingers were all battered, and the tip of two of them was missing.

I gasped with shock. 'You were beaten?' I said.

He nodded. 'Those bastards hit me with a hurly stick. But Marina, I don't want to talk about it. Not now. Really, I don't.'

'When did you get out?'

'Five years ago – the minute I was 16 I was thrown out of that place with nowhere to go. And the first thing I did, Marina, was to look for you. I was told you were in England. I looked for you there, but there wasn't a trace of you.'

'Well I was never there. Never,' I said.

'I know that now,' said Philip. 'I begged Uncle James to tell me where you were. I was sure he knew, since he had organised things when you left the county home, and when our grandmother died too. And finally he said you were in the laundry. But when I went there looking for you and asked the nun who answered the door to fetch you, she said, "There is no Marina Byrne here." Then she slammed the door in my face.'

'That's terrible,' I said, upset to think how close he had been to finding me.

'I rang the bell again,' said Philip. 'And I asked her again. And eventually she said, "I think you mean Fidelma." And I said, "but I don't know a Fidelma." Then she shut the door again. When we went back the other day, we had to threaten Mother Scholastic with a solicitor or she wouldn't let you go. But Marina, when I saw you I *didn't* know you. You are so thin. Did they feed you at all?'

'The food was terrible,' I said. 'And there was never enough of it. We would faint from the hunger.'

'Looking at you, I think, if you had been in that place for a month or two longer you would have died,' he said.

Later, Philip told me more about his time in Artane. He had been nearly killed from the beatings. There were terrible marks all over his back. I cry whenever I think about it – about what they did to Philip.

My Uncle John allowed me to live with him and his wife in their house on Talbot Street in Wexford even after Philip had returned to work. That gave me a semblance of security, yet I felt unsettled. I was free, but I was still living in fear. I was frightened to go anywhere.

My younger brother, Seamus, was living with my Uncle John too. He had been with another uncle – one who had thirteen children, but he wasn't happy there and ran wild in the fields, so after his marriage, Uncle John collected him from his brother.

I met a girl up the road called Moira who was good to me. One evening she said, 'There's a bit of a dance on Marina. Will you come with me?'

I nervously agreed, but soon worried what I would wear. I had no nice clothes and no money to buy anything with. Philip said, 'I've got some spare cash. I'll buy you a dress.' Philip was a catering officer on the *Oriana*. He had worked his way up to that. I was very proud of him.

Moira collected me, admired my new flower sprigged dress, and off we went. We walked into the hall, which was large and bare with a wooden floor, and the band was playing up one end. I blocked my ears, because after the silence of the laundry the music seemed so very loud. The men were all lined up on one side of the room, and the women were on the other side. We stood with the women, trying to look as if we were enjoying ourselves. Then this dark, handsome boy came across to us. I thought he was going to ask Moira to dance, but he came and spoke to me. I was terrified, because I didn't know him from Adam, but Moira gave me a push and said, 'Go on Marina.'

We were real innocent. We danced, then we talked a bit and he told me his name was Sean. He was friendly, and had a lovely smile and blue-grey eyes. Then we danced again, and I felt less self-conscious, and let the music wash over me. I began to really enjoy the evening.

He told me that he worked in the town and I said I needed a job. He asked me what my last job had been, and I felt frightened all over again. I didn't tell him I had been in the laundry. I was scared to. I didn't tell anyone, not for years and years. I was ashamed.

I had thought of telling Moira, but Philip said she would get the wrong idea. 'She will think you've had a baby, Marina,' he said. 'Or that you are a fallen woman. Everyone thinks that's why girls get sent to those places.'

So I didn't tell. I didn't want anyone knowing.

Sean didn't kiss me that night. And the next time we met at a dance he didn't kiss me either. But he said he wanted to see me again. I wanted that too. I liked him but I was surprised that he liked me. I always thought of myself as an ugly duckling.

I wanted, more than anything, to work as a nurse. Or anyway, to work in a hospital, but there weren't jobs for the likes of me. It was the farmer's daughters who got the jobs. Not poor people. I didn't know what to do. Then one day I was looking through the *Catholic Universe* and I saw an advertisement. It was calling for Irish girls to work in a hospital in England as orderly nurse assistants.

I told Sean about it, and he encouraged me to go. He said, 'I'll miss you Marina, but you have to put yourself first. And maybe, in a while, I can come and join you.'

I was so excited! I told my uncle, and I applied. My uncle lent me five pounds, which I paid back as soon as I could, and before I knew it I was on the train and boat for England. As I stood on the deck of the boat leaving Rosslare Harbour, I watched Ireland become further and further away, until I could no longer see land. And I thought, at last! I'm off to England, and away from those nuns forever.

CHAPTER 22

MARINA

IT WAS A hard journey, and a long one, and I was exhausted by the time I got to London. I was frightened to death too.

I got off the train at Paddington Station, and found myself carried along in a sea of people towards the ticket barrier. I thought I'd be squashed to death. It was a huge station, and there were all these announcements about trains about to leave for places I'd never heard of. The echo was terrible. Looking around helplessly, I didn't know where to go next. I asked a man how to get to the station for Banstead in Surrey, where the hospital was, and he led me down some steps to the Underground. It was like the tunnel in the laundry, only worse. There was so much noise from the trains. And when the right one arrived, and took off into the underground tunnel, I nearly lost my life with fear!

The hospital was a psychiatric hospital. Despite the suffering I witnessed, I enjoyed my time there. I had a way with the patients. If they were in a bad state they were given shock treatment. They hated that, and would not get on their beds when the doctors and nurses asked them to. So I would hug them, or dance with them round the floor, and they would get on their beds with no bother. I had a great way with all of them; everyone said so.

When I had been there for a week, I was given some money. My first ever pay packet. I will never forget that, after all the years of working for nothing. I had to pay for my lodgings out of it, and for new stockings, and there wasn't a lot left over, but I always saved a little. My Uncle John taught me that. He would say to me, 'Marina, put a shilling away for a rainy day.' And I did.

There were 5,000 patients in Banstead, and there were a lot other psychiatric hospitals in the area. I think it was because of the war. A lot of the men who had fought suffered mental health problems, and women suffered with their nerves.

I loved Banstead, but after a while, in about 1955, I decided to go to London. I had been writing to Sean in the year since I'd left Ireland, and I wanted to see him again. He had a sister living in London, and he said he was going to visit her and try to find a job.

There were lots of jobs in London. And nobody bothered if I was Protestant or Catholic, they just gave me one. I started off working in a laundry, because I hadn't any confidence and that was something I knew how to do. It wasn't so bad. The work was hard, but it was nothing like the Magdalene laundry. I worked on the calendar, pressing the sheets and people were nice to me. Unlike at New Ross, they were friendly.

It was hard to find lodgings. There were a lot of rooms for rent in Kilburn, but there would be a notice saying, 'No blacks or Irish need apply.' That shocked me. In the first room I got, in Kilburn, the landlady was fierce strict. It was 'no boyfriends allowed'. That was hard.

When I was 21, Sean and I got married. He seemed a good man. I liked him, and I wanted the security. It was nice to have someone, because for years I'd had nobody.

We were happy. Well, at first we were.

I wanted children, I always had. So when I found out I was pregnant, I was over the moon. Sean was too. But one evening when Sean was out drinking, as he so often was, I had a terrible pain and I started to bleed. I was so frightened. I called the doctor, who came to visit me in our rooms in Kilburn. But he said, 'I'm sorry to tell you, but you've lost the baby.'

CHAPTER 23

MARINA

I BECAME PREGNANT two more times after that, but I suffered more miscarriages. The third time Sean came home to find me lying on the floor, not able to move. He called an ambulance and I was rushed to St Mary's Hospital, Paddington. I nearly died, and never got pregnant again. I try not to dwell on it too much, because if I did I would go mad.

I was so unhappy afterwards. I was severely depressed, and I couldn't see a way out. Sean was out drinking all our money. He had a fierce temper when there was drink on him. And one day I decided I could take no more. I waved my husband off to work, put all my clothes into a bag and went to stay with an uncle in Paddington. I didn't tell anyone at work. I was too ashamed. The attitude in those days was, 'You made your bed now lie on it.' Nobody would feel sorry for you.

On a number of occasions Sean would try and find me, to make me go home but I was scared at what he might do. My nerves got so bad. And one time when a friend, Patricia, visited from Ireland she said, 'Marina, you can't be frightened of him all the time. You have to get a divorce.'

She was right, so I filled out the paperwork and travelled to the West End for the hearing. I felt so terrible, and feared I would never have the strength to go through with it. I thought, 'I will go home with Sean. It will be easier that way. I just can't get divorced. It will cause me so much shame.'

Sean wasn't there when I arrived at court. He wasn't there when I went into the witness box. He didn't see me crying and crying when the judge asked me questions, and he didn't hear the judge tell me that I was a very brave and wonderful woman for staying married to Sean for as long as I had. It wasn't that he was so very violent, but I'd told the judge of my constant fear.

Sean never showed up, and I did go through with it. But I couldn't stop shaking, because divorce was such a terrible thing in those days. Especially if you were a Catholic, and came from Ireland where there was *no* divorce. I didn't visit Ireland for years after that because of the shame.

A stranger approached me afterwards. He had got his divorce that day too. 'You look like a lovely woman,' he said. 'Let me take you for a cup of tea?'

I said I wouldn't. I said, 'I just want to go home.'

'Please?' he said. 'Or if you don't want to come with me now, can I contact you later? I'd love to see you again.'

'I'm sorry, but no thank you.' He looked nice enough with his neatly cut hair and his smart suit, but I didn't want to have anything to do with men, never again.

Soon afterwards I went to work in Smith's factory in Cricklewood. We made components for cars. I got on well there and would look after the new workers, buying them a roll from the trolley until they got their first pay packet. I was always kind. That's my way.

The supervisor, William, used to look at me and smile a lot. It made me blush. One morning as he passed by he said, 'I'm going to marry you one day.'

I just laughed, thinking I'm not going to marry an old fellow like that who wears glasses. I was frightened to death of getting married again. But we stayed in touch.

I was alone for 16 years after my marriage ended. I didn't have boyfriends; not like they do today, but I saved my pennies and went out to dances. I used to love going to the Irish dancehalls in Kilburn where I lived, or to the Galtymore in Cricklewood. You would have a laugh and a mineral drink.

We would arrive in a group; there was a great gang of us Irish in Kilburn. Often there would be more women at the dances than men, and we'd stand around the edges like wallflowers. Then when the pub closed at about 11 o'clock, the men would stagger in. They would have a good few drinks on them.

Sometimes, you would see one coming over towards you, and they could hardly stand up.

'Would you like to dance?' they'd ask, their speech slurred.

'No thank you.'

'Well if you're not dancing, why didn't you bring your mother with you?'

That made me laugh. Another night when I refused a man, he said, 'What are you doing here if you're not dancing? Why didn't you bring your knitting?' The poor fellow was falling all over the place, and I'd had enough of that with Sean.

All that time I stayed in touch with William, or Bill, as I now call him, the supervisor from the Smith's factory. And he waited for me. He waited until my nerves were not so bad. And when

I was 40, we married. I moved into his cosy flat, complete with central heating. I was in heaven.

I didn't stop work when I married. If anything, I worked even harder. In the day I was working at the GEC factory, which made washing machines and fridges. Getting up at 6.30 a.m., I'd work in the factory all day on piecework. I was in charge of a line. I'd get back to make dinner for Bill. Then later I would meet this friend, Mary, who came from Sligo, and we would go out to work again, cleaning the office of an Irishman for a couple of hours.

'You're such a worker, Marina,' my boss used to say. 'You're a white tornado.'

I think it came from the nuns. I could still hear Mother Scholastic saying, 'The devil makes mischief for idle hands.' Her words rang in my ears. I could never forget them. Even now, I keep active round the clock. I'm never idle for a minute.

At GEC we could get a discount on the machines, so after a year of marriage I bought a washing machine, because Bill said I should. But when it first arrived I was frightened to death of it because it reminded me of the convent. I still hate machines. Bill bought me a microwave five years ago and I have never used it. Not once.

Bill was very good to me, and I felt safe with him. So safe, that I risked telling him about the laundry. I watched his expression, worried he would think worse of me and believe that I was a fallen woman, but he took my hands in his and said that a terrible thing had been done to me and I should try to forget all the horrible things the nuns used to say. 'You're a good, kind woman, Marina,' he said. 'The kindest I have ever met. Everyone knows that.'

It felt wonderful to unburden myself in this way, and it helped me so much knowing that he was on my side, but my nerves were still bad. I could never forget how unkind the nuns had been. I suffered bad bouts of depression, and I still do.

Sometimes, when cooking the Sunday roast, I'd think of my mother, and of her leaving in the ambulance. I'd think about the laundry, and about Philip too, who had been beaten so very badly in Artane, and I would burst out crying. Bill would put his arms around me and hold me until I felt better.

Bill is from Swansea but, when he was 65 and retired, we decided to come back to my roots in Ireland. I had lived in England for 36 years.

We returned to Wexford town, but at first I hated it! I could not settle. Living back there reminded me of my poor mother and of all the times we went hungry. It made me sad all over again.

After a while I joined the St Vincent de Paul Society, and the Stroke Club as a volunteer. This helped me enormously. I would sit with people and I could really relate to them. It was good to learn about other's lives, and the difficulties in their pasts. I visit people in hospitals too and all the people I've met have become good friends.

I always hoped I'd meet some of the girls who had been in a laundry with me, but I never did. I did meet a woman who remembered it though. She was a friend of my granny's and she owned the ass and cart that took me to my confirmation. She was now very old and I would do her shopping for her on a Tuesday.

I told her I had been in the laundry, and she gasped with shock. 'I can't believe it,' she said. 'Fancy! I used to walk by that building every Friday, and to think you were in there.'

Philip can't forgive the Church for what they did to him in Artane. He was so bitter that he emigrated to Australia to get away. He won't set foot in Ireland; he didn't even apply to the Redress Board. He couldn't face it.

I try not to rage at the nuns because anger makes my nerves bad. I look at it all from both sides of the fence. I think life was funny back then. I would not give up my bit of religion for anything. I go to Mass and I thank God, every day, for all the grace and blessings he has bestowed on me. Sometimes I get disheartened, but I always hope God is up there. I love the Sacred Heart and Our Lady. It's a comfort.

All I want is my health and peace of mind. Some days I feel I have that, and some days I don't. Looking after Bill, who is 90 now, can be stressful. He can't do much, and I can't stop. When I try to relax, and watch TV maybe, I hear Mother Scholastic's voice in my head. She's saying, 'The devil finds mischief for idle hands.' I can never, ever forget that.

CHAPTER 24

STEVEN

MARINA GAMBOLD HAS changed so much since the day I first met her at the screening of *The Forgotten Maggies* at the SGC cinema in Dungarvan, Waterford. One of the first members of Magdalene Survivors Together, I have watched her grow in confidence ever since.

Before Waterford the documentary debuted at the Galway Film Festival, but it had been a struggle to get the film shown. With no budget, myself and the cameraman Ger Boland had worked through many days and nights editing down reels and reels of film. I remember freezing in my unheated London flat. I'd wake every morning at 6 a.m. and lie in bed listening to the women's stories. This went on for three years, and then the festival turned it down. I was in despair. Then I picked myself up and decided to give it just one more try.

After a massive re-edit, I travelled to Galway where I staged a 'protest' to make the festival organiser change his mind. I had never before been so determined, but it felt like the right and only thing to do. So, after all those problems, it felt something of a miracle when it was shown. I was determined to take advantage of its monumental success there.

We were now showing *The Forgotten Maggies* in all the counties where there had been a Magdalene laundry, and Waterford was the first stop. I hadn't advertised the screening; I couldn't, because I had no budget. I'd given up my job in London in order to concentrate on the documentary while my parents were getting pretty pissed off paying my enormous phone bill. Despite the challenges, Waterford was a great screening. It had sold out; there were 450 people in the audience and there was a phenomenal reaction to it. We had the longest ever applause and the place was buzzing.

Standing outside the cinema afterwards, with my family and friends, I was happy. I had made a documentary that told the story of four women. The press had picked it up, and I had been invited to give a screening in New York. I felt the survivor's stories were out in the world, and my job was done.

Then this woman burst through the doors, bawling, crying, the tears flowing down her face and everyone turned round and looked at her, wondering what was after happening here? She was a small woman with round glasses sitting on her nose. She had white hair and wore a pink jacket, which was half zipped. She was visibly upset.

'I was one of those ladies.' The words burst from her lips. 'I was in a laundry. Everything I saw in that documentary happened to me.' She took out a tissue, removed her glasses and wiped her eyes. 'I'm Marina Gambold. And I have been trying for years to get compensation. I went to the Redress Board and was turned down. I know what it was like.'

I looked at her thinking holy fuck! There is another woman who needs help. This is *not* over.

The realisation left me feeling distracted. I gave her my

The Child of Mary ceremony at Stanhope Street School, May 1950.
The girls had to look smart to make a good show in public.
Kathleen is on the back row, fifth from the left.

The laundry at St Mary's claimed to be a training school. Many girls fainted as a result of the sweltering heat and steam rising from the enormous machines. Kathleen attended here aged just 14. (Pat Cotton)

Right Kathleen as a little girl, on the main road in her home town of Lisvernane, Co. Tipperary.

Below Marie as a little girl, preparing for her Holy Communion in a dress bought by her grandfather.

Top right A newspaper advertisement for the 'industrial training school' at St Mary's. None of the children were ever paid for the work they did.

Right Certificates were issued by the religious order telling families about the exams the girls were sitting. Kathleen says they never took place and that the report was made up to give a false perception of the institution.

Industrial Training School for Orphans and Children of Respectable Parents.

ST. MARY'S **LAUNDRY** STANHOPE ST., DUBLIN.

AND WORKROOM.

Conducted by THE SISTERS OF CHARITY.

Contains over 100 Children; in receipt of no Governmental or other Grant.
Orders taken in Workroom for Gentlemen's Shirts, Ladies' Blouses and Underwear.

Laundry Work for Families, Hotels, Colleges and Religious Orders also REPAIRS at Lowest Prices.

Vans call for and deliver all Orders in City and Suburbs. Tel., Dublin, 1408.

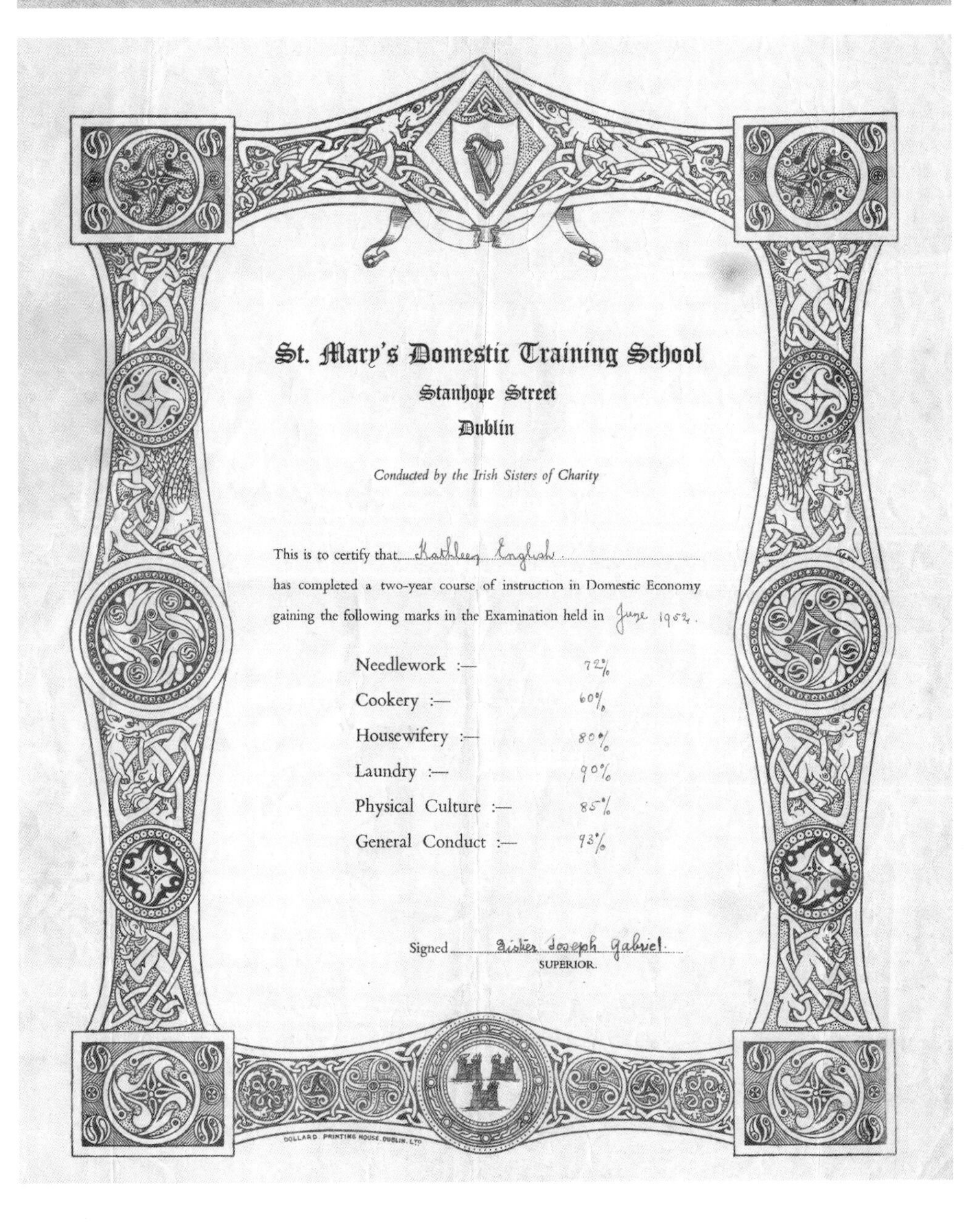

St. Mary's Domestic Training School
Stanhope Street
Dublin

Conducted by the Irish Sisters of Charity

This is to certify that Kathleen English
has completed a two-year course of instruction in Domestic Economy
gaining the following marks in the Examination held in June 1952.

Needlework :—	72%
Cookery :—	60%
Housewifery :—	80%
Laundry :—	90%
Physical Culture :—	85%
General Conduct :—	93%

Signed Sister Joseph Gabriel
SUPERIOR.

DOLLARD PRINTING HOUSE DUBLIN. LTD

Exhausted faces in the hot laundry room, where religious paraphernalia hangs above them on the walls. (Pat Cotton)

Diane, aged 15, in Dublin.

After working in Rotunda, Kathleen took a job with the Women's Royal Air Force, where she ended up meeting her future husband, Robbie (pictured right).

After 52 years, Marina visits the Good Shepherd laundry in New Ross. She is stood on the steps where she was first told her new name was to be Fidelma. (Jim Crean)

Opposite Nancy was just 10 or 11 years old when she went to a Magdalene laundry. Aged 22, after years of abuse and tragedy, she finally found safety and contentment through her work caring for children. *Top:* With Leo and a neighbour. *Below:* Nancy playing happily with the children in the garden.

Right Diane as a baby, being held by her mother who was just 16 when she gave birth.

Returning to Stanhope. This was the first visit since Kathleen had left all those years ago. The site of the former Magdalene laundry is now a home for the homeless. It's a place of hope, goodness and, as Kathleen describes it, a garden of peace.

Marina, Steven, Kathleen and the Lord Mayor of Carlow. This was taken at the Carlow march in 2009 when hundreds of people came out to support the women.

phone number and told her to ring me anytime she liked. Her little face fell. So I said, 'Look, we're having a march in Carlow. Why don't you come along to that?'

She managed a smile and said she would, then the woman she was with put an arm round her shoulders and led her away.

Kathleen flew over from England for the march in Carlow. It was one of those fresh autumn days when there's a crispness and a brightness hovering over everything. There were a lot of local counsellors there, and we made sure to dedicate the day to all the women who had been in school, laundries, and mother and baby homes. There was a real sense of purpose.

It didn't feel political though. It was so jolly and friendly, there was a lovely spirit of unity. The Magdalene women were finally coming together to do something for themselves. They were transforming from victims, and were now tearing down the walls of silence to become survivors with a cause.

A woman approached me and said, 'Hello Steven. Do you remember me?' and I realised it was Marina. She looked different this time; well, she was a lot happier and smiling.

I introduced her to the other women. She and Kathleen took to each other at once. They have become firm friends, and write to each other regularly. That feeling of well-being increased as we marched, carrying the huge banner, planted a tree, released doves and a big bunch of balloons.

I flew to New York the next day for the screening at the Cantor Film Center, on behalf of Glucksman Ireland House. The screening was sold out, and the Grammy-winning musician Julie Gold was there. The American audience reacted very vocally to the film. They were so furious that they shouted at the screen. They were interested in the subject in a different way from the Irish because they were more removed from the subject matter.

In Galway and Dungarvan, where the community had been badly hurt, there had been a sense of 'these are real women, and they don't fit the stereotype. They could have been my cousins.' The Americans' sense of shock, though just as genuine, felt less personal.

After the performance in New York I was buzzing. I rang my mother and she said, 'The women are all over the news here.' The broadcaster RTE had come to cover the Carlow march and filmed a clip for the news. Joe Duffy had then picked up the subject for *Liveline*, Ireland's most popular phone-in programme and Magdalene women rang in in their droves.'

Then I received even better news. The Irish television channel TG4 wanted to screen an extended version of *The Forgotten Maggies*. I set to work making that, adding Marina Gambold to the cast. It was hard, because I had to raise the funding myself. I did that by taking part-time jobs, and I kept costs low by persuading everyone who was part of the production to give their services for free.

I brought Kathleen Legg back to Ireland too. We returned to the village where her grandmother lived and she saw her grandmother's grave for the very first time. I'll never forget watching Kathleen that morning, as she stood reading the inscription on the tombstone in that windswept graveyard. Memories poured out, and she cried, thinking of all the people she had once known. It had been 60 years since she was in her home town and the village she once knew had been long lost.

Then we took her back to Stanhope Street, which was now a charity centre for homeless people. She looked around, amazed, recognising parts of the building, but confused by the changes. Watching as the emotions flitted across her face, I thought,

What an amazing woman Kathleen is. She is so dignified, and carries herself so well.

We had achieved so much, but there was still a long way to go. Now that I knew these women, and knew their stories, I felt an obligation to help them. And that meant getting the state to recognise that they had been dealt an injustice.

Many of the women had applied to the Redress Board hoping for compensation but had been turned down. Kathleen was told that Stanhope Street was a training school and not a Magdalene laundry, and others were turned down because the Redress Board only covered Industrial Schools. The problem was that once the women had applied to the board they were unable to re-apply for any future compensation. For the ones who had been turned down that was, obviously, totally unacceptable.

I thought of several ways I could raise the women's profile. I wrote to the Department of Justice in the hope that they would meet the women. I didn't expect that they would agree, but on 4 November 2009 I took five women along to meet with the then secretary general Sean Aylward. He listened to the women, and we got great media coverage; that was essential.

When, after a few months, the issue of the Magdalene women had dropped out of the public gaze, I decided we should have an anthem. I got hold of all the great musicians I knew, including Daniel O'Donnell and Sinead O' Connor, and persuaded them to record a charity single. I was delighted when Julie Gold gave us permission to use 'From a Distance', her Grammy award-winning song. It didn't sell millions, but it was fun to do and it kept us in the news.

The funds raised from the venture went towards creating a monument dedicated to all the women who were incarcerated in Ireland's Magdalene Laundries. This gave the women an extra sense of purpose.

Next, I approached Frank Buttimer, a solicitor, in the hope that we could make a constitutional case, but he said that could take an extremely long time. I was worried that most of the women would not be alive to see it through. One had died since I started working with her, and we simply hadn't got time on our side.

We started down the legal route for the women, but it was an uphill struggle, and after a year of hard work the women were getting restless. There was talk of taking complaints to the Gardaí but that, I believed, was clutching at straws.

I tried everything. I wrote letters to anyone in Dáil Éireann who I felt might help. We had meetings with the departments of education, health and environment. But I began to feel that politicians were just pretending to be interested in the women. Next, I contacted the Irish Human Rights Commission, but to no avail. Everyone claimed that the state was not involved in the running of these institutions. They said they were run by the church.

Going home to Cork for Christmas in 2010 I was starting to despair. It was, anyway, a gloomy time in Ireland. The Celtic Tiger boom, which we all assumed would continue forever, was becoming a distant, golden memory. The banking crash at the end of 2008 had changed everything, and the country was now in deep recession, each year worse than the one before. The Fianna Fáil government under Brian Cowen was in crisis. Nobody trusted them anymore. It was a joke.

And in that climate, with everyone worried about their jobs and the country's survival, nobody seemed to care about the Magdalene women. We wondered if we should perhaps take the issue to the European Parliament.

Then a general election was called and, on 25 February 2011, the electorate voted in a new government, leaving the Fianna Fáil party in tatters. We were now led by a Fine Gael, Labour coalition under Taoiseach Enda Kenny. Fine Gael had been helpful around the Magdalene issue when they were in opposition, so I saw this as a new opportunity and decided to target the new government cross party committee. Kathleen Lynch, the new Minister of State for Disability, Equality and Mental Health helped gather a meeting of ministers, and they made us some promises.

In May, Secretary General Sean Aylward was flown out to the United Nations to talk about torture, and the subject of the Magdalene laundries came up. He told the UN that according to the evidence, women had gone to laundries voluntarily or been placed there by their families. He mentioned meeting some Magdalene women, but said that as far as he could recall none of them had been placed there by the state. I realised he was talking about our women, and wondered whether he had been listening to their words at all.

His statement was simply not true. Marina, as an orphan, was essentially in the care of the state; so was Diane Croghan, a new member of our group, who, abandoned in a county home at birth had later been sent to Summerhill laundry in Wexford town. There were many other women in the same predicament. That statement made my blood boil.

Then my luck changed. I was given a ledger from a Magdalene laundry in Dublin which showed that various state bodies were involved in the laundries. These included the Department of Fisheries, the Department of Justice and Áras an Uachtaráin. This proved that the Magdalene laundries were not private. I also came across files showing that the Department of Health funded the Magdalene laundries, paying a capitation grant of £1 a week for every Magdalene woman. The state surely *had* to accept responsibility.

In July 2011, *The Forgotten Maggies* aired on Irish TV. It won high praise for its honesty, and increased public awareness. We were on a roll! More and more women came forward. We now had 25 members within Magdalene Survivors Together, and we started to hold monthly meetings in Dublin.

During that summer of 2011, Kathleen Legg rang me with some bad news. She hadn't been feeling well for some months. The last time she had visited Ireland we had all noticed that she was short of breath, and pale too. On returning to England she had contacted her doctor; he had performed scans and diagnosed lung cancer.

I was really upset. The longer I had known Kathleen, the more I respected and liked her. She was 75, and it was as if she was my grandmother. I couldn't bear the thought of her dying before she had received a state apology. I felt, after she had trusted me enough to tell me her story, that it was my responsibility to make sure that an apology happened, and soon.

Once the Dáil's summer recess was over, I got hold of the Department of Justice again, and Minister Alan Shatter said he would like to meet the group.

I wrote down all the women's stories, and told them they had 10 minutes each to talk. We went round the table and the women were superb. They told their stories in a powerful, emotional way. You could sense the shock in the room. And then we came to Kathleen Legg.

She looked frail that day. She had been through a course of radiotherapy and was not expected to live much longer. I had worried about bringing her to Ireland, but she was determined to come. And when it came to her turn, she started to cry.

'All my life I have felt like an alien,' she said. 'I worked in Stanhope Street, and the state has told me it was a training school. Do they think I don't recognise a laundry? Do they think I imagined working on a calendar, from nine in the morning until five at night? Don't they know that I carry the shame? I didn't tell a soul that I had been in a laundry. Not one person. I kept it a secret for almost 60 years. I thought if I told my husband he might walk out on me.

'I lived in Ireland all my young life, but when I applied for an Irish passport I was denied one. I am now a British citizen. And when I applied for a pension, I was told I was not eligible for one, because nobody except the Rotunda Hospital ever paid for a stamp for me. As far as the state is concerned I do not exist.

'I now have cancer. I am suffering. I am in pain. The cancer is eating me up.'

Her voice shook, and I feared she would break down. But taking a deep breath, she continued, 'I don't expect to be here next year. I am terrified that I will die before the state agrees that my story is true. I won't live to hear an apology.' I had never heard Kathleen speak with such raw emotion. She clearly thought she must take this chance to let her feelings show. When she had finished, there was dead silence. It was as if the ministers were shell-shocked. No one knew what to do. Then Shatter thanked the women warmly, and congratulated them on telling their stories so well.

Looking at these innocent women, many of whom were never educated, some who could neither read nor write, and who didn't understand life, I thought what a phenomenal way they had come. By speaking out they were transforming their lives.

When we first set up the group, I don't think they knew what to expect. But then neither did I. We all just went along with the journey. We were fighting; we were campaigning; they had now been interviewed so often that their faces were becoming well known. In becoming articulate, they were empowered. They were listened to. And in that moment, I knew we had turned a corner.

CHAPTER 25

STEVEN

AFTER THAT, THINGS rolled along nicely. Martin McAleese, husband of the former president, Mary McAleese, was selected to compile a report. I met him and felt he was the right choice. I trusted him, and was sure he had the women's best interests at heart. I liked the other appointee, Nuala Ní Mhuircheartaigh, too. She was deputy permanent representative of the UN, dealing with human rights. Over the course of the process we developed a good, friendly working relationship.

We arranged for the women to meet Martin McAleese in December 2011 in Government Buildings. The women were bubbling with excitement when I told them. Kathleen was unable to attend that day, she was undergoing radiotherapy for her cancer, but Marina was among the chosen group who met the media. The stewards greeted us, welcoming the women with wide smiles and showing us into a side room. It was clear they really wanted the women there. As for the women, they felt like film stars and they loved it! They fell onto the tea and sandwiches, and were impressed to be presented with name badges.

'I wish those nuns could see us now,' said Diane, with a wicked grin.

After a while we were taken to the meeting room. The high-walled corridors were lined with portraits of past heroes like Michael Collins and President de Valera. It was hard not to be impressed with the opulence of the building and the sense of history it evoked.

The women were riveted, especially when they spotted some well-known members of Dáil Éireann. There were cries of recognition. 'There's Mary Lou McDonald,' said Diane. Marina spotted the new minister of agriculture. 'Ah look,' she said, her eyes bright with excitement. 'There's Simon Coveney. Isn't he a lovely, lovely man!'

They became a little quiet when we entered the meeting room and took their seats round the large table, but there's something very gentle about Martin McAleese. His demeanour relaxed the women. He seemed genuinely glad that they were there.

'Thank you for coming to see me,' he said. 'It's very good of you. And I understand some of you have had to travel a fair distance.' He said he knew it would be hard for them to tell their stories, and to revisit the pain of the past. 'Just take your time,' he said.

It was an emotional afternoon, as these meetings always were. Some of the women spoke of extreme abuse; one, just a child, had been stripped naked and beaten time after time. Another had made numerous attempts to escape, only to be dragged back by the Gardaí to face increasingly severe punishments.

I got a strong sense that Martin and Nuala believed the women and wanted to do all in their power to help them. We left that day feeling pleased, and that at last something was about to happen. But there was one major problem. Stanhope

Street, where Kathleen Legg had been kept, along with several other women, was not being included in the report. Neither was Summerhill, where Diane had spent two years. They were both still classed as training schools, even though each institution had a laundry where the 'pupils' worked six days a week.

McAleese asked to meet each of the women again, each one alone. He was good to them; he just wanted to gain clarity of their stories, and confirm all the details. Meanwhile there were so many phone calls between him and me, and also with Nuala, and in each one I pleaded, 'Please include Stanhope Street and Summerhill.'

McAleese told me I could see the report before it was made public. And true to his word, he sent it. I was on the main Irish radio show, RTE I's *Today* with Pat Kenny on the morning it was coming out. That is the premium show that could, I felt, influence things. McAleese hoped I wouldn't leak details of the report, before it was read in the Dáil that afternoon, but I had my own agenda.

I started with the positive points. I said that Martin McAleese had been a compassionate listener, and that I felt he had taken the women's stories on board. I explained the issues; that the women wanted apology, compensation and pension rights. Then I got to the crux of the matter.

'Some of the women are disappointed,' I said, and he asked why. 'Two laundries were not included.'

'And why is that?'

I explained about Stanhope Street and Summerhill; about how they were supposed to be training centres and he said, 'Sure, I was at school in Stanhope Street. I remember there was a laundry there. I distinctly remember the smell of the sheets.'

I felt I'd hit the jackpot. I explained that Dublin's High Park, also a training centre, had been included, so why not Stanhope

Street and Summerhill? We then talked about the women's expectations of the report.

I decided we should not be in the Dáil to hear the McAleese report. I thought it would be more useful to set up a press conference outside, so that we could report to the world. We set up at the George Frederic Handel Hotel near Dublin City Council; I alerted the press, then stopped answering my phone to ensure that the media came to us. And they did. We chose Marina, Diane Croghan and two other women to talk to the press, and kept the rest of the 26 survivors, who had declined media attention, upstairs. The women told their stories. They were, as always, amazing. I was thinking, 'This cannot get any better.'

We knew the report confirmed that the state had placed women in the laundries. This was true of over a quarter of the women who were estimated to have passed through the 10 laundries; either through court orders, the social services or through the industrial schools. So we were waiting for the news that the Taoiseach had said sorry.

Then a BBC reporter, having heard an update from the Dáil, said that the Taoiseach had said he was *not* going to apologise on behalf of the state. I was stunned. I didn't know what to think, but the women were simply pissed off. And they weren't afraid to say so. They were so visibly upset that I decided to bring the press conference to an end. I turned to the press and said, 'If Enda Kenny can stand up in the Dáil and criticise the Catholic Church in Rome about the Cloyne Report, then what I'm wondering is – is this Magdalene Ireland or is this the Republic of Ireland? These women, and I'm sure the wider society at large, would like to see an official apology and closure. His refusal to admit blame on the part of the state is a complete and utter cop out.'

*

The following day the papers were full of it. The headlines screamed: 'Magdalene Survivors Expect Unreserved Apology.' Meanwhile RTE interviewed Kathleen Legg on the phone from Bournemouth, bringing the issue of Stanhope Street back to the fore. We were on a roll.

President Higgins appeared on the news, being interviewed from Rome. He said as far as he could see this was a Human Rights issue. The women had been detained against their will, and their forced labour had not been remunerated. Micheál Martin, leader of Fianna Fáil, got on the bandwagon too, slamming Enda Kenny. He said he should say sorry 'with no ifs and no buts.' The Labour Party and Sinn Féin joined the calls for an apology.

The following week, Magdalene Survivors Together offered Taoiseach Enda Kenny an olive branch. I asked for a meeting. After a lot of negotiation, we organised that he should meet six of the women, including Marina. So it was back into the Dáil, to his private rooms. They were treated like royalty and felt like superstars. Marina, in particular, adored that day.

'I loved Enda,' she told me. 'He came up to me after the meeting, and said I was a great woman altogether. He said I was very strong. I never thought of myself that way. I never was, but since I started telling my story, since the group, I feel different. More confident in myself. He kissed me on the cheek.' She blushed. 'I took his hand, and I said, "I hope life for you and your family will be full of hope and goodness."'

The following day I had arranged for Marina to appear on Ireland's most watched and longest running talk show, *The Late, Late Show*. Marina and a friend travelled up to Dublin together, and we were all put up in a hotel close to the RTE studios. They sent a car for us, and we went together with another survivor. A researcher met us in reception and took us up to the green room where all the other guests were assembled.

Marina didn't like the look of the sandwiches. 'They're too fancy,' she said. 'Why can't they just give us cheese or ham?' I just laughed, and soaked up the atmosphere and the buzz.

Marina was shaking with nerves. Then it was time. And she and the other woman left the green room, heads held high.

She was wonderful on that show. She praised Enda Kenny, saying what a nice man he was. 'He said he wanted to put a face to the report,' she said. Then she told her story, mentioning the cup she wore round her neck for three days, and her stint out on the balcony. She mentioned her lack of confidence, instilled because the nuns always told her she was nobody and would never be anybody. 'But then I met Steven,' she said, 'and he made us all believe anything is possible in life.'

She had the audience in tears. When the presenter, Ryan Tubridy, asked if the Taoiseach was going to apologise, she said, 'Yes. There's going to be an apology on Tuesday.' Watching in the green room, I cheered. I had asked her to say that, to make absolutely sure that the Taoiseach would not go back on his word.

When Ryan Tubridy asked her why an apology was so important, she talked of her sense of shame. 'I was very hurt by the nuns,' she said. 'You're called a fallen woman, but I never had a child. The only time I fell was from hunger.' Her voice broke and the tears came.

'Well you're standing tall tonight,' said Tubridy. 'You have changed things tonight. You have told your story and it has brought the Magdalene story alive for us. We can't wish you enough happiness in future.'

*

The day of the apology everything came together. Our group had expanded to 30 women by then. As we walked to take our seats in the front row, Nuala Ní Mhuircheartaigh tapped me on the shoulder. 'You're going to be happy today Steven.'

'Am I?'

'Yes,' she said. And she winked. 'You're going to be very, very happy.'

When Enda Kenny spoke there was silence in the Dáil. He recounted the women's stories with genuine regret. He announced the setting up of a review to work out compensation for the survivors under Mr Justice John Quirke. I waited with bated breath, until, finally, he spoke the words I had waited to hear.

'The McAleese Report also refers to women who recounted similar experiences in other residential laundries,' he said. 'Such as the laundry offering services to the public operated in the training centre at Stanhope Street, Dublin.' I waited for him to mention Summerhill, but he didn't, and I realised my job was not yet done. Even so, I was over the moon. This meant I had not let Kathleen Legg down. I took my phone out of pocket. It was switched off, but my fingers itched to dial in her number, so that I could give her the good news.

Enda Kenny's apology to the Magdalene women was broadcast all around the world. It touched people so much, and was picked out by several newspapers as one of the most important events of 2013. Afterwards, my phone never stopped. Survivors came forward from all around Ireland – 165 in all - wanting to join the group. I promised each of them that I would do all I could. Some of their stories would break your heart.

I thought I had heard it all. And then one night, when I was watching the RTE news over a cup of tea, my phone rang.

'Is that Steven O'Riordan?' It was a woman's voice.

‘Yes,’ I said.

‘Are you the one who is helping the Magdalene women?’

‘I am.’

‘Well Steven, this is Nancy. I’m ringing from Galway, and I want to tell you my story.’

She began to talk, and once she had started, it seemed she was unable to stop. I listened to Nancy in increasing horror as she told of a lifetime of abuse. By the time she had finished my tea was stone cold, and I was crying.

CHAPTER 26

NANCY

I was 10 or 11 years old when I went to a Magdalene laundry. Just a child. The nuns said I had to go there because I was a troublemaker. But I wasn't. Not really; not like some of the other girls. I still don't know the real reason why they sent me.

I was in fourth class at the Mount orphanage in Limerick. We were out in the playground one day when there was a fire drill. I was up on a swing and my best friend, Emily, was on the swing beside me. When the fire bell pealed, we were up, up in the air, and it took a few seconds for the swings to slow down enough so that we could get off.

Emily got down before me, and she ran off in a big hurry. Then she started to scream. I thought she must have fallen over and hurt her knee, then I noticed she had her arms wrapped around her head. And the nun, Sister Maria, was shouting at her.

'You are too slow,' she screamed. 'Imagine if this was a real fire? You'd be burnt to a crisp by now.' The nun kicked Emily, and I realised it was she who had hurt Emily. She had whacked her, and banged her head off the wall. I watched and I was frightened. My swing was still going too high and I couldn't jump off. What would Sister do to me?

Sure enough, by the time I got over there she was really mad. Her eyes behind her glasses looked wild. She caught me by the hair and knocked me against the first step. My chin split and blood spouted out. I screamed in agony, and she shouted at me to shut up. 'Look what you made me do!' she screamed. 'When will you ever learn to do as you are told?' Then she pulled an old white hanky out of her pocket, threw it at me, and told me to hold it to my chin.

She shouted out to a woman who helped the nuns – they were called mountresses – 'Take this wretched child down to Barringtons Hospital,' will you,' she said. 'She's made a terrible nuisance of herself.' She didn't say sorry. But then the nuns never did. Not ever. I looked back to see if Emily was okay. She was sitting on the step now, still holding her head while Sister was saying, 'Get up now. Stop crying. There's nothing whatever wrong with you. You haven't a cut like Nancy.'

We walked through Limerick. It was the first time, ever, I had left the orphanage gates. I had often wondered what it was like in the city, but I wasn't in the humour to enjoy it. My chin hurt me, and the blood was streaming down my neck. It was going down my frock too. I worried what the nuns would say about that. The mountress didn't give me any sympathy; there was only one thing on her mind.

'Don't say the nun did it,' she said.

'But she *did* do it.'

She slapped me and, yanking my arm, dragged me along the pavement. 'If you do tell, the doctors won't believe you. Because I'm going to tell them that you fell.'

When we got to the hospital, the helper gave my name at the

desk. Then we sat on these plastic chairs and waited. We waited for a long time. My chin hurt, and the sight of the blood scared me. Then a nurse said it was my turn and she led me into the doctor. The helper followed me in.

'This is deep,' said the doctor, and he dabbed at my chin with cotton wool. It stung and I cried out. 'That's just antiseptic,' he said. 'I'm making sure it's clean before I stitch it.' Then, picking up a needle and thread, he said, 'What happened to you?' I was so scared about that needle going into my chin that I forgot to lie.

'The Sister did it,' I said, and the helper put out her hand to slap me. Then, realising that wouldn't look good, she said, 'Don't listen to her. She fell. She's just a troublemaker.'

The doctor raised his eyebrows but said nothing. When I was all stitched up, he put a big plaster onto my chin. 'All done,' he said. 'You can go home now.'

I wished that I was going to a *real* home – and not back to the orphanage. There was a little boy running down the corridor in front of us, with his mammy chasing him, telling him to stop. And I thought, if I had a mammy I would never try to run away from her.

My chin still hurt. I wouldn't have minded so much, but as the helper dragged me along the pavement, she hissed, 'You'll be for it now. Just you wait until I tell Sister Maria that you blamed her for this!'

I *was* for it.

Sister Maria called me a liar. 'You tripped. We all saw you.' She was spitting with rage. 'And anyway, who would believe you, just an orphan?'

I was dragged up the stairs and locked in a tiny room, like a cell. I had never been in trouble like this before. Not like some of the girls who were always being beaten. Yet now they were treating me like the worst person in the world, and all because I'd told the truth. If I'd kept my mouth shut in the hospital, perhaps I would have escaped all that was to come.

CHAPTER 27

NANCY

I DON'T KNOW where I came from, or who my parents were. I was found lying in a basket in a grotto in the Mount orphanage in Limerick. Back then, in the 1930s, babies were regularly left there. Or so the nuns said. 'You're not so special Nancy. There were many other babies found there, besides just you.'

The orphanage was an industrial school, and it was full of unwanted babies and children. Some were orphans, like me, and there were others whose mothers were fallen women. That meant they weren't married. They said my mother must have been a fallen woman, but they didn't know that for sure.

The nuns knew nothing about me. They didn't have a record of the day that I was left there, so I don't know my age and I don't have a birthday. That makes me really sad.

They called me Kathleen Macgregor. They said the name had been written on a piece of paper pinned to a blanket in the basket I was found in. I don't know if that was true because when I was baptised, much later, the certificate said I was Kathleen Ritagen.

I didn't wonder who my mother and father were when I was young, because I didn't understand how families worked. I didn't know how babies were made. I thought, *Maybe God leaves babies in the grotto?*

Some of the children in the orphanage had a mother or a father. Others had both. A few had brothers too, but they would be in a boys' orphanage. Sometimes the mothers or fathers would visit their daughters, or take them out for the afternoon, and the rest of us would be so jealous. They would come back with bags of sweets. They would unwrap the papers and suck them in front of us, but they never gave any to us. That made us cry, but the nuns never told the girls they should share.

The bigger girls would try and take the bag of sweets when nobody was looking, but they never got away with it. Someone would always tell on them, and then they would be beaten. I robbed some sweets once. A girl in my dormitory had been out, and I saw her put a paper bag in her bedside locker. I wanted those sweets so much. I was thinking about them all morning when we were in the school, doing our sums.

I told Emily, and she said, 'Well let's get them then. Nobody will know.' So after lunch we slipped off when no one was looking. We crept up the stairs, went into the dormitory and took the whole bag. Then we went into the toilets and ate them, one by one. They were boiled sweets, I remember, and they tasted so good. But when the girl found out that they had gone, she told the nuns.

'Who did that?' she thundered.

I didn't say anything, but I looked at Emily and she looked at me, and we both went red with the guilt. We were whacked over the hand with a stick. It hurt badly, and I never robbed sweets again.

Some of the girls got lots of beatings. I didn't get too many because I was scared of the nuns and always tried to please them, but that wasn't easy. They always found something that I was doing wrong. I wasn't walking fast enough or I didn't know my lessons. They didn't even need a reason to push me around or slap me across the face. They knew I had nobody. They could do what they liked.

There was a nursery in the orphanage for all the babies and toddlers. I must have been there when I first arrived, but I don't remember it. The nursery was a noisy place, with babies screaming. There was a smell in there too, of damp and sour milk.

We ate in a huge refectory out of metal bowls that wouldn't break if we dropped them. There was lumpy porridge every day for breakfast. It was horrible, but we ate it because we were always hungry. We had tapioca sometimes which we hated even more.

We slept in great big dormitories with beds down either side of the room. The worst thing you could do was wet the bed. To stop us doing that the nuns made us get up in the middle of the night and line up to go to the toilet. If you still wet your bed, they would take up the mattress and stick a piece of paper on it with your name on so everyone knew what you had done. Then you were made to wash your own sheets.

When I was old enough I went to the orphanage school. They told us stories like 'The Three Little Pigs', but I didn't learn to read or write. We were crowded into that classroom. Sister Catherine would walk up and down, looking at our work, but she looked after some girls better than others, and she didn't look after me. She would just glance at my work and sigh.

There was a beautiful big doll's house in the Mount school. It was like a real house, but we were never allowed into it. It was only there for show, for when visitors came around. I can remember one lady coming in, looking at it and saying, 'Look at that! Aren't you lucky little girls?' If only she knew. The truth was that we didn't have toys to play with, not anything, unless you count the rag dolls we made for ourselves. The nuns showed us how to twist worn bits of fabric around to make a body, heads, legs and arms. Then we sewed eyes in with black thread.

After school we were made to clean the orphanage. We would be down on our knees scrubbing the floors and cleaning all the skirting boards until our little arms ached. Some evenings we had to go and clean the church and the cloister, polishing the pews. It was hard work, and we were only small. The nuns were Mercy Sisters, but there wasn't anything merciful about them. Some of them were nicer than others, but they were all domineering. They thought they were being so good to look after all of us unwanted children, that they didn't think they had to be nice. Our mothers were seen as sinners because they had a baby without being married. I didn't understand that then. But I did learn one thing: I was worth nothing.

At Christmas we went to church. We knew all about baby Jesus whose birthday we celebrated on Christmas Day. I thought, *Isn't Jesus lucky to have a birthday?* I wished I had one too.

Santa didn't come to the orphanage. There was no Christmas tree or decorations. But one year we had crackers to pull. That was so exciting! But when we pulled them we didn't get a hat or a little toy, just a little bit of paper.

Not long after Christmas I woke up and my skin was on fire. I was tearing at myself. I could feel these creepy-crawlies coming down my neck. There was no way I could sleep. I was roaring crying, and the nun on duty marched over to me.

'What is it, child?' she said, stripping off my bedclothes and hauling me out of bed. 'You'll wake the dead with your noise, so you will.' She shook the living daylights out of me.

Then, seeing me scratch at my head, she had a peek, sighed, and dragged me into the bathroom. She pulled at my hair with a fine comb. She was rough as she yanked out the knots. All these creepy-crawlies were falling into the water, and I felt sorry for them. That was the nature I had. That wasn't the first time I had lice and it wouldn't be the last; they came crawling out of our hair or our nightgowns would be swarming with them.

One summer, Sister Maria said I was going on a holiday. I was very small and wasn't at all sure that I wanted to go. But when this woman came to collect me, I thought, *She seems nice.* She smiled at me, told me her name was Mrs Costello and cuddled me. Nobody had ever had done that before.

She lived in a lovely village called Adare. When we arrived, she took me upstairs and showed me into a little bedroom. There were only two beds in it. I slept in the smaller one. It seemed strange being in a room all by myself, but I liked it and I liked Mrs Costello too. She had a grown-up son who had become a soldier but she lived alone. I had a lovely time there and Mrs Costello would take me to the shops. She asked me about my life in the orphanage and took me with her to visit her friends, and they were kind to me too. I ate cakes and biscuits. We never had those in the orphanage, except maybe once a year.

Mrs Costello was the first person, ever, who seemed to like me. I went to her for a week in the summer for two or three years. I loved her. She was like a mother to me. She used to call me Nancy, even though in the convent I was Kathleen. When it was time to go back, I would plead, 'Please can I stay here? Please keep me.'

She would hug me, but say she couldn't. 'It's not possible, I'm so sorry. You have to go back.'

It was terrible to return after those two short weeks of bliss. And it got worse every year. I'd know what it felt like to be loved, then that love would be taken away again. It was like giving away a pet after a few short weeks of enjoyment.

I was looking forward to her taking me out again. This time I truly thought she was going to take me for good. But I never saw her ever again. She had died. I missed her so much I had an ache in my heart. I had lost the only person who had ever cared about me.

CHAPTER 28

NANCY

After the incident with the swing, I was left in that cell for a week and a half. I thought I'd go mad. There was nothing to do and nobody to talk to. The room was bare except for the bed. The only I time I saw a living soul was when my meals arrived on a tray. But the person bringing them didn't speak to me. I felt so lonely locked up there, and my chin still throbbed.

I thought I would never get out of that room when, after 10 days, the key turned in the lock and there was Sister Maria. 'Off you go to the refectory,' she said. 'And have a cup of tea.'

I didn't need telling twice. I was so happy to get out of there. I ran down the stairs, through the corridor and into the refectory, then sat down with my tea and some bread and jam. I'd only had two bites when Sister appeared, puffing, and telling me I should not have been running in the corridor. 'Hurry and eat up, or you'll miss the bus,' she said. I thought, but you've just told me off for hurrying. It didn't make any sense.

I didn't dare speak my mind and instead said, 'The bus? Am I to go on a bus?'

Sister nodded. 'You're leaving us, Kathleen.'

My mind was spinning. 'Why?'

'Why *Sister*,' she huffed. 'Because we can't keep troublemakers like you.'

I felt so angry at those words. I had tried, so hard, always to be good. And I didn't want to leave the only place I'd ever known. I was sad to be leaving Emily too. I wanted to go and find her, to tell her what was happening and to say goodbye, but Sister Maria had other ideas. I remembered times when other girls seemed to disappear. We had always wondered where they had gone. Would they be in this place I was going to? Would I now disappear too?

The mountress who'd taken me to the hospital came and told me to put on my coat.

'Hurry,' she said, looking at her watch. 'The bus leaves in 15 minutes.'

I didn't know where I was going, and I was scared. And I never, ever saw Emily again.

The helper lady was a demon. She was so angry all the time it would frighten you just to look at her. I sat on the bus with her. I looked around at all these people: the old men, the women in their headscarves and the little boys with their scabbed knees, and I was frightened. I was only used to little girls and nuns. When I heard anyone talking, I would look round and stare at them, and the lady would pinch me and tell me off.

I rubbed my arm and said, 'I think I don't like you.'

'And you think I care?'

I don't know how long we were on that bus, but it felt like hours and hours. The further we went, the more frightened I was. I began to cry. 'Where am I going?' I sobbed.

'Ah, you will know soon enough.' She was grinding her teeth

and making a fist. She seemed very cross, but then she always did.

'This is our stop,' she said, when the bus reached a road lined with golden leafed trees. She dragged me off the bus. I had no luggage with me. I didn't have anything to call my own. No clothes, except for the raggedy ones I had on me. We walked down one long street, then up another one, crunching through fallen leaves. I still had no idea where we were going, but then I saw these huge big gates.

'Here we are,' said the lady, smiling now. 'You are landed.'

There was something about the way she said this that made me scared for my life. I ran across the road, screaming, but she chased me and dragged me back by my hair.

We walked up a long, long drive with trees down either side, and came to a huge redbrick building, with three parts to it.

'This is a Magdalene laundry,' she said.

I didn't know what a laundry was, let alone a Magdalene one, so I asked her and she laughed.

'It's a place that will sort you out once and for all – you and your nonsense,' she said.

I started to shake. The helper knelt down, and stared into my face. 'You wouldn't want to tell the nun here that I pulled your hair now, would you?' she said. 'Because you know, now, what happens to little girls who tell tales?'

'Why are you talking to me like that?'

She sighed, and just looked me up and down. 'And if you think being locked away for 10 days is a bad punishment, you wait and see what you will get in here.'

She rang the bell and this nun with a stern expression answered it. They spoke on the doorstep for about five minutes, then the lady went away and left me standing on the doorstep. She never even said goodbye. She left me there like a dog.

I watched her walk away, thinking that for all her cruelty I'd rather be with her going back to Limerick than staying here in a place I didn't know.

I will never forget the nun's first words to me. 'Well, we have another black sheep for the family.'

I didn't know what she was talking about, but I later learned that these were the Good Shepherd Nuns. So as 'sinners and fallen women', or the children of fallen women, we were the black sheep.

'Your name will be Bernadine,' she said.

'But I'm Kathleen,' I said, though I now thought of myself as Nancy. I had done ever since Mrs Costello started calling me that.

She stared at me, and said, very slowly. 'We can't call you Kathleen because we already have a Kathleen here. Do you understand? So you are now Bernadine. Your number will be 23.'

'Alright Sister,' I said, my voice squeaking like a mouse.

'It's *Mother*,' she said. 'And don't you ever forget it. And let me tell you, Bernadine, we won't have any of your disruptive behaviour here, is that clear?'

'Yes Sister. I mean Mother.'

'You will do what you are told, and you will come when you are called. Do you understand *that* Bernadine?'

'Yes Sis—Mother.'

'This is God's house. Everything you are told to do here, you will do.'

I didn't question her. I knew nothing that was going on in the world, so I thought this was the way I had to live.

CHAPTER 29

NANCY

THE NUNS SAY that I arrived at the Good Shepherd Sundays Well Magdalene laundry in Cork in 1949. But their records weren't in good order, and that can't be right. I think it must have been four or five years later. I had been in fourth class, so I would have been nine or ten, and that date doesn't make any sense.

The first thing that Mother – her name escapes me so I'll call her Monica – did was to take me to a big room, with glass all the way round it, that she called the ship. There were shelves and shelves of clothes stored there.

She handed me a brown frock made of horrible stiff material, and told me it was my uniform. It came down to below my knees. She gave me a white apron to go over it, and some old black shoes that were worn and too big. 'You'll soon grow into them,' she said.

Next she cut my long hair up to my ears, and gave me a band to keep my hair neat. Looking at my long brown hair fall in clumps on the floor, I felt sad. In the orphanage, we used to wind our hair around brown paper, and tie that with thread, so when we took the paper out we had ringlets. I couldn't make ringlets now.

Mother Monica was very cross looking, and didn't seem at all pleased to have me there. I was miserable. I didn't know what to say.

'Come now, and I'll show you where you'll be working,' she said, dragging me down some corridors to a room where lots of women were scrubbing clothes. Nobody said, 'Hello'. Nobody said a word. I didn't know why.

'This is a mangle,' said Mother Monica, showing me a noisy machine with big rollers on it. 'You will get your turn pulling the sheets out of the washer, and then you will put them into the wringer. And you will get your turn folding the sheets with another girl, and putting them into a big roll, and you will stand with another girl pulling at the sheets and folding them again, and you will do this several times until the sheets are dry. Then the sheets will be folded again. You will get your turn doing all of this.' She made it sound as if I was in for a real treat, but the women in the room didn't look one bit happy.

Next she showed me the dormitory. This wasn't so different from the one in the orphanage. There were about 20 beds, but this time we had curtains between each one.

I hadn't been happy at the orphanage, but at least I knew the other girls. Here, I didn't know anyone. When Mother Monica said I was to be in Miriam's circle, I didn't have a clue what she was talking about, but I knew soon enough.

There were 12 women in every circle. The head of the circle, Miriam, was an auxiliary. That meant she had been in the laundry for years and years and was more holy than we were. She wore a bonnet on her head, and she was treated better by the nuns.

Everyone in the circle was a different age, but none of the others were nearly as young as me. We ate on a table with our circle, we were in a dormitory with them and we sat together after tea to do recreation.

There were very old women in the laundry, and there were some girls my age, but the nuns kept us apart. There were also older girls who would be crying because they wanted their babies. I never saw babies in the laundry, but the building the other side of the main convent was a school called St Finbarr's. When we went to the chapel, we were kept on the right-hand side, with the nuns in the middle, and the children from the school on the left. We could hear the nuns chanting in Latin, but we couldn't see them – except, maybe, for the top of their heads. We couldn't see into the other parts, but the girls who had children in the school tried so hard to see. They'd stand on a pew when the nun wasn't looking, but they never could see over. It made them so sad they would sometimes cry.

The nuns kept telling us that we were penitents. And as part of our penance, we had to live in silence. And if you dared to open your mouth, even to whisper, you would have to stand at the servant table for three days. The silence was hard to get used to.

There were a lot of penitents in Sundays Wells. I'd say there were over 100. But not all of them were working in the laundry. Some of the women were sewing, making priest's vestments. I'd say some of them had been there all their lives: some even died there.

At the time, being so innocent, I didn't understand why anyone was sent there. I didn't know what a fallen woman was. The nuns called them prostitutes sometimes, and said maybe my mother was one. I didn't know what that meant either.

Some girls were sent in because their families didn't want

them. One girl wanted to be there. She said it was better than being at home because her father beat her so badly. I met a girl, later, who said she was sent into a laundry at 15 for no reason at all.

We would be woken up at 6 a.m. every day. First thing, we had to go to Mass. We had no tea, and nothing to eat before Mass and often we would feel weak. Sometimes we fainted onto the floor, but we had to get up again. Fainting was never an excuse; however bad you felt you still had to get on with your work.

After Mass, we would go to the refectory for breakfast. It was lumpy porridge every day. Then we could have bread and dripping. The dripping was the grease off the nun's meat. I never complained about the food. I didn't dare. Some girls did, but it didn't do them any good. They were given a beating in front of us all. I remember watching one girl as the nun laid into her. She didn't cry or shout out, and that made the nun so cross that her face went redder and redder. Watching, I was trembling with fear. Sometimes girls were sent away and we never saw them again. One minute they were there, the next they weren't. We never knew where they went.

When breakfast had finished, at about 8.30 a.m., it was time to start work in the laundry. We would work hard all morning, heaving sheets in and out of the machine, doing whatever we had been asked to do.

The sheets came in from the North Infirmary, the South Infirmary, the Imperial Hotel and Parknasilla Hotel. Those were some of our biggest contracts, but a lot of local people would send in their clothes to be washed too. There would always be lots of shirts.

The girls in the packing room sorted through the laundry, making sure all of it was marked. It was washed, and then put onto presses. You might do the front of the shirt; someone else would press the back and another person would do the sleeves. We would pass the shirt on, one to another.

We had a break at dinner time. I think that was around midday. We would get something like black pudding and mash. I never ate my black pudding. I hated it. I remember one day the girl sitting alongside me couldn't eat her dinner. She whispered to me how much she hated it, then she took a handful of mash and said, 'I'm going to give the nuns some work to do now.' She threw the mash onto the ground, shouting 'North, south, east and west,' as she threw it in different directions. She was much older than me. I thought she was so brave.

She gave me this cheeky grin, and I laughed. Mother of Our Lady looked down from her throne and saw us, and there was all hell to pay. We had to stand at the servants' table for three days. She stood at one end and I stood at the other. And all because I laughed. It's no wonder I never dared to talk.

After dinner we had to go back to the laundry until about 6 p.m., and then we would have our tea. Sometimes we might get a fried egg, but we never got a big fry-up; I don't remember ever seeing a sausage. There was never enough food. Some girls would go into the refectory at night where they would rob the place of bread because they were so hungry.

When we had finished our tea, it was time to go into the recreation room and sit in our circles. Miriam had to make sure the rest of our circle did our work, making things for the nuns to sell in their shop. We made scapulars, which were pieces of cloth joined by string to be worn over the shoulder to show devotion. We embroidered the initials 'BVM' on them which stood for the Blessed Virgin Mary. We had to sew on her image too.

We also made scapulars for St Anthony's Blessing. I still

remember the blessing. It was: 'May the Lord bless you and keep you, and make sure his countenance shines on you, and may he take pity on you, and may he turn his eyes towards you and give you his peace.' I must have made at least 1,000 of those during my time there. We made rosary beads too, and holy pictures.

When we had finished our work it was 9 p.m., and time for bed. We'd wait for our number to be called, then go up to the dormitory and change into our nightgowns, putting them on before we started taking our clothes off. That was so we could stay modest.

Before we could get into bed, we had to go down on our knees. The nun on duty would walk up and down the dormitory saying, 'Hail Mary, full of grace, the Lord is with thee.' Then she would shout out another prayer. To this day I have never forgotten the words. It was, 'Good night sweet Jesus, Lord and saviour, this night thy beauty I will see, in this blessed hope, goodnight sweet Jesus, I want to go straight to sleep to dream of thee.' Then, without taking a breath, she would say, 'Not a word! Don't let me hear any of you talking; you know it is your penance, and you should not talk.' She would walk up and down like a sergeant major.

When I first saw that we had these green curtains round our beds I thought it would be nice. And if we could have drawn them when we wanted to be alone and then open them again, it might have been. But it kept us separate, so that we could never make friends. We never dared to talk. I'd go to bed lonely, and wake up lonelier still. There was no one in the world who cared for me.

CHAPTER 30

NANCY

IT WAS VERY hard to keep clean in the Magdalene laundry. In the mornings we might only have time to give our faces a quick wipe. And we only had a bath maybe every two or three weeks. We had to queue up and all use the same water. There would be all this frothy dirt on the surface, and by the time it was my turn the water would be cold.

One time I got this terrible rash and would scratch and tear at my skin. In the morning my bed was full of blood, and in the day there was blood all over my sleeves. It didn't go away for a long time.

I didn't know the facts of life when I was in the Magdalene laundry, and neither did I know about periods. When I got my first period I hadn't a clue what was happening. I was terrified when I found blood in my pants and thought there was something really wrong with me. I told one of the sisters (I can't remember her name but will call her Frances), and she took me down to the linen room. She gave me a big thick sanitary towel made out of material. They made them themselves. There was a loop at each end, and they gave me a belt to put the loops through to hold it up.

'When you finish with it, you must put it into this wash bag,' she said, showing me a huge bag hanging on a hook there. 'And you can take a new one.'

It was a horrible thing. It was all stiff, and there was such a terrible smell coming off it. Now I know the smell was from the bleach they had to use to get all the bloodstains out. The sanitary towels rubbed, and made me all sore. Even then, the nun did not explain to me what the bleeding meant. She didn't tell me that women bleed every month. I expect she was too embarrassed. And I never heard about periods from the other girls either. That's the trouble when you are not allowed to talk.

We never left the laundry, it was like a prison. But sometimes we would be taken for a walk around the grounds, though we were carefully guarded. There would be a nun behind us making sure we kept walking on. Part of the grounds were wired off, and some days we would see women on the other side of the wire. When they saw us, they would run over and clutch at the netting, crying.

'We're locked up,' they would sob. 'We're locked into cells by ourselves, but we haven't done a thing wrong. We're sick, that's all. We have TB.' I felt sorry for the women, and wanted to stay and comfort them, but the nun would shout, 'Walk on now. Quickly! Walk on.'

Their cells were in a different bit of the building. We only saw those women when they came outside.

When I first arrived at the laundry I noticed some girls wore long dresses, right down to the ground. I thought to myself, *Those dresses must be nice and warm*. But I was soon to realise that the women were wearing them as a punishment.

There were apple trees in the houses round the convent, and

the branches hung over the wall into the grounds. When the apples were rosy and ripe, they sometimes fell onto the ground. One day, I was very hungry when we were outside. I thought nobody would mind if I had an apple. If I didn't have it, the birds would eat it.

So I picked it up and put it in my pocket. But Sister Frances saw me, and she snatched it out of my pocket and flung it over the wall screaming, 'This doesn't belong to you, Bernadine. It doesn't even belong to the convent. And you must not steal from the convent's neighbours!'

She made me wear punishment clothes for a week. And that's when I realised how horrible those dresses were to wear. They were hot, heavy and itchy. The nuns treated you worse when you wore punishment clothes. And wearing that dress made me feel ashamed.

I tried and tried to be good in the laundry, because I wanted to become a Child of Mary. Everyone wanted that! You had a special Mass, and afterwards you had a slice of cake and some biscuits for tea. You were given a blue rosette to wear, with a medal in the middle. It meant you were senior in the laundry. It took at least five years to become a Child of Mary.

You had to earn the rosette. After my first year in the laundry they gave me a green ribbon with a medal on it. I was so happy. But it took me a long time to get the next ribbon, a purple one, because of the apples and the talking. I wondered if I would ever become a Child of Mary.

It was very hard not talking to the other girls, but we were afraid for our lives. Once, a girl was talking in the laundry and when the nun came down to her she got up and tore the veil off the nun. I couldn't believe my eyes! She was taken away and we never saw her again. I wonder if she went to the asylum.

The nuns were always talking about the asylum. They would

threaten us and say if we did anything wrong, that's where we would go. I didn't know what it was, but I knew it must be a terrible and frightening place. I think a lot of girls did go to the asylum. They were sent when they got fits of crying, or when they refused to do their work. I once heard a nun say to a young girl, 'You're going to the asylum, and you won't get out ever again.'

We were allowed to talk on Christmas Day, and also on the Feast of the Good Shepherd. The priests of the Good Shepherd would come and say that we could talk, because we were the black sheep, the penitents. They were always saying that, and saying, 'Do your penance.' They made sure that we said our prayers.

It was all very well being allowed to talk for that one day, but the trouble was when we hadn't talked for so long we didn't know what to talk about. I turned to the girl beside me in the refectory, and said, 'Where are you from?'

'From Cork,' she said. 'Where are you from?'

I didn't know what to say. I didn't want to tell her that I was from a grotto, so I said, 'I'm from Limerick.' We didn't say anything after that.

CHAPTER 31

NANCY

ONE DAY, WHEN I had been there for ages – over a year – I woke up with a pain in my mouth. I thought, *What am I going to do?* After breakfast, when we were cleaning the orphanage, the pain nearly drove me cracked. It got worse as the day went on. I was working in the ironing room then, and it got so bad I couldn't take it anymore. I turned to Mother Margaret and said, 'I have a terrible pain in my face.' I was nearly sobbing with every word, because it hurt so much to speak.

She just looked me up and down before turning away, saying 'Get on and do your work.'

'But I can't.' My face felt so bad that I had to hold it in my hands. I was crying out with the pain. My ear felt bad too. I had never felt agony like it.

'You are working today,' she said. 'If you still have the pain tomorrow, we will see about it then.' The pain went on all day. It got worse and worse, and I couldn't sleep that night.

The next day Mother Margaret sent me to the infirmary where I was told I needed three teeth out. But I didn't think it was my teeth hurting me. It was my face, and looking back I think it was neuralgia or earache. Miriam, the auxiliary who was head of my circle, came down to the dentist with me. While we were walking there, I thought maybe I could get away from her. It was an instinctive reaction, because I'd never dreamed of escaping. I wouldn't know where to go. But I started to run, and she caught me. She was mad angry. When we got to the dentist she sat close beside me, and when the dentist called me in she came in too.

'Where is the pain?' he asked.

'It's my face,' I said. But Miriam cut in over me,

'Don't listen to her. That's just her imagination. She needs three teeth out.'

The dentist was a brutal man. He put this great big needle in my mouth and then he yanked my teeth out. Having the teeth out was very sore.

Afterwards my face was still paining me. And the pain didn't go away. It was still there a week later, and after another week the pain had spread to the other side of my face.

I couldn't stand it anymore and I went back to Mother Margaret and told her. She sent me straight back to the same dentist. When Miriam came to get me, she had this length of wide band. It was binding and must have been cut from a worn sheet. I recognised it as a sheet from the Imperial Hotel.

'Give me your arm,' she said. I put out my arm, and didn't she tie the band round my wrist. She dragged me to the dentist like a dog.

'You are hurting me,' I gasped, and she was. She was walking really fast, and I had to run so that I could keep up.

'But you can't get away, now, can you?' There was triumph in her voice.

'I hate you,' was all I could think of in reply. She just laughed, and pulled even more roughly at my wrist.

That time the dentist pulled out seven teeth. You can't imagine how sore that was. I felt dizzy and faint, and it was terrible hard walking back.

When I got back to the Magdalene laundry I was sent straight back to work, but I felt awful. I begged Mother Margaret, 'I am very sick. My mouth is bleeding all the time. Can I go and lie down please?'

'Get back to your work Bernadine,' she replied, sternly.

'But the blood . . .'

Sighing, Mother Margaret brought some cloth over to me, and shoved it, roughly, in my mouth. I cried out with the pain. 'That will keep the blood in,' she said. 'Now, no more excuses. You've got time to make up.'

So I went on ironing that shirt, with my mouth was full of cloth and blood. The blood went back into my throat, and I couldn't help but cough it up. Some spluttered onto the shirt. I was crying with the pain, and worried I would choke. Mother Margaret, noticing, came over and thumped me, hard, in the back.

'My word, Bernadine,' she said. 'That is the priest's sacred shirt.' She took a step or two back, and said, 'Hold out that shirt to me.' I did, and she sprinkled holy water on it.

'Get down on your knees, girl.' She pushed me down on the ground. 'Kiss the floor, and say, three times, "I am sorry for putting blood on the priest's sacred shirt."'

I did that. Then I had to wash and scrub all the blood out of the shirt. And all this time I could taste the blood and feel it trickling down my throat. It was terrible. My punishment was to take all the clothes out of the washer. That should have been someone else's job. And all the while all the other girls were looking at me like dummies. Because, of course, they couldn't talk.

When my mouth had healed, the pain in my face had still not gone away. So I had to go back to that dentist for a third time. And when he had finished with me I had very few teeth left.

Afterwards I had all these clots of blood coming out of my mouth. And when that stopped, I would wake up and there would be a terrible taste in my mouth. It was hard to eat without my teeth. I used to dip my bread into my tea. When they were all out, my face was still paining me. But it went away after a while.

I cry every time I think about losing my teeth. It breaks my heart. All those teeth gone, and there was nothing at all wrong with them. It's as if it wasn't enough to take away my childhood and my freedom. They had to take my teeth too.

CHAPTER 32

NANCY

ALL THAT TERRIBLE hard work, and we were never paid a penny. Not one. I've heard people say that the government was paying the nuns to look after us, but you would want to see the amounts of money that was arriving in the van. I remember seeing a big biscuit tin with piles of notes all tied together in bundles with elastic bands.

There were few good times, but the day I was finally made a Child of Mary, when I'd been in the place for around six years, was one of the better ones. There was a special Mass, and we had a piece of cake for tea. I felt privileged that day, and happy. But it wasn't to last.

It's not surprising, with the terrible way we were all normally treated, that some girls tried to escape. I never did, not seriously. I wasn't brave enough, and I had nowhere to go. But there was one girl who had been talking about escaping since the day she arrived. I was 18 by then.

This girl, Lilly, was three beds away from me in the dormitory. She'd arrived in the orphanage a week before, and she had hardly stopped crying in all that time. She was pretty, with fair hair, and she was crying for her baby. She had been bawling all evening, but the nun who was saying the prayers at bedtime didn't care at all. She said, 'Tears won't help. You will never see your baby again, but you should be pleased. He now has a good, Catholic home, and parents who can give him a happy life. What could you, a *sinner*, give him?'

That girl said she was sick. Her breasts were sore. I didn't know it then, but I think her milk must have been coming in.

She was so desperate to see her baby, didn't she make a rope by knotting all the blankets together? I watched this, and wondered what she thought she was doing. When she opened the window from the bottom, tied the blankets to the metal of her bed and put them through the window, I rushed over and said, 'Be careful.' But she brushed me away.

Then she climbed out of the window. I begged her not to go, but she said she would slide down the blankets to the ground. I believed her. She swung down and I held my breath, but the blankets didn't stretch far enough. We were six flights up, and she fell the last three flights. I heard the thump as she hit the ground, and I cried out in shock. Some other girls ran over. We looked down, and saw her lying on the ground like a broken doll. I saw it all, and I heard her terrible scream. Then I heard the scream in my dreams.

We never went to her funeral. And the nuns didn't talk about her at all. Her name was never mentioned, but I never forgot her. Not ever.

I couldn't get Lilly out of my mind. I was so upset, thinking of her and the baby she had loved so much, that I didn't know what to do. The next time I went to confession in the convent chapel, I decided to talk about the way I felt. There was a Redemptorist priest hearing confessions that day. I didn't normally like confession, because I never knew what to say. I'd think, *God, what am I going to say at all?* I would be making something up. I'd say that I was disobedient, even though I wasn't. But after the girl had died, I said, 'Father I am very sad.'

'What are you sad about my child?'

'That I am in here. Could you get me out of here please?'

There was a long pause before he spoke. 'But there must be a reason for you to be here, my child.'

'No,' I said. 'There isn't.'

'You have to do your penance.'

'If you don't get me out of here, I'm going to try and run away. I am!' My outburst surprised me; I hadn't realised how much I needed his help.

But he didn't take any notice. He just sighed, and said, 'You have to stay here my child and do your penance. And for your other penance, now, say one Our Father and three Hail Mary's.'

'Yes Father.'

'And then say the act of contrition. God bless you.'

And to think I was expecting some consolation from him!

I did try to escape. I tried to climb over the wall, but there was glass stuck into it and I couldn't manage it. I never tried again. And nobody saw me trying to escape. I was lucky.

Each girl got a turn packing the laundry, and when in the packing room we would see the vans coming in to collect the clean laundry and drop the dirty sheets. A lot of girls escaped in the vans, but they were almost always brought back again by the Gardaí.

Lilly's death upset me so much. I couldn't stop thinking about it. I didn't feel like doing anything. Maybe I had depression? I don't know. When they didn't want to work, some girls in the laundry would go 'on the ran' and they'd sit on the stairs for a few hours by themselves. They were always punished, but they still did it. I don't know why.

I didn't do that, because I didn't want to get into trouble. I'd go into the work room as usual, but not do my work properly. I refused to eat too. I became very weak. I think the nuns were getting a little afraid of me. One day Mother of Our Lady marched up to me.

'Bernadine, are you going to eat?'

'No. I'm not,' I said, crossly. 'I don't want to be here.' I'd never answered back in my life, but I'd gone past caring.

She looked at me in astonishment. 'Well, Bernadine, there is only one cure for you.'

I had no idea what that 'cure' would be. But knowing the Good Shepherd nuns, it couldn't be anything good.

CHAPTER 33

NANCY

MY CURE WAS to be sent to another Magdalene laundry, this one in Waterford. My records say this was June 1957; I'd arrived in Cork eight years earlier – but I don't believe anything I read in those records. I think the nuns made them up.

They sent me packing with just the clothes I was standing up in. Before I left I said, 'Can I have my coat please?'

'What coat would that be, Bernadine?' asked Mother Monica.

'The one I arrived in.'

Mother Monica looked me up and down, then she said, 'Don't be silly! That won't fit you now.' So I had to travel on the bus without a coat. I was so frightened to be going to another laundry. I imagined it would be terrible, because the nuns said I was being sent there as a punishment.

I was roaring crying for the entire two-hour bus journey. I felt desperate, and didn't know what to do. I'm sure all the other passengers must have been staring at me, wondering what was wrong. But nobody said anything. I thought I was going mad.

They were still the Good Shepherd nuns in Waterford. I did all my work but I was miserable. I was even more unhappy than I had been in Cork. It was worse, because the nuns were desperate cross. You'd be afraid to even look at them. They didn't use my name there. Not Nancy, not Kathleen, nor Bernadine. They just called me by my number.

We had the same bread and dripping, and the same work. We were slaves. But the laundry there came from the hospitals. When we sorted the sheets they would be covered in blood and intestines, stuff from operations. A terrible smell would come off them as we handled them. We were never told we could wash our hands. It was desperate.

I was so angry and upset when I arrived in Waterford. I would burst into tears which slowed down my work, and I couldn't stop shaking. I still wasn't eating, and I became very weak. I was going off my head. I would try to work, and I'd manage bits and pieces like ironing a shirt, but then I'd get dizzy and I would say, 'I can't do this anymore.' My arm couldn't hold the iron any longer.

I couldn't sleep and kept waking up in the night. One night I woke up and thought there was a man running after me with a knife. I screamed, and a nun rushed in and began to slap me, telling me to be quiet.

'Carry on like this, and you will be locked up in the asylum,' she said, but I was so scared about the man with a knife that I kept on screaming. She shook the living daylights out of me.

The nuns kept threatening me with the asylum. That scared me, because a lot of girls were sent to a mental home when they threw fits or tried to get out. And once you went into one of those places, you never got out again. Or that's what the nuns said, anyway.

One time, I had my turn with the big gas iron. It was heavy

and hard to manage. You would light the first jet, and then tip the iron so that all the other jets lit, one by one. Then the whole lot were alight. On this occasion I burned my wrist on the iron and it went into a huge big blister. Then the blister burst. I showed the nun, but she didn't care. Nobody did.

A few weeks later I was ironing and this girl beside me felt faint. She sat down and put her head down between her knees. She was very pale and shaking.

'I'm going to die,' she groaned. I knew her to look at, but realised I didn't even know her name. How could I, when we were never allowed to talk?

I put up my hand to get the nun, Mother Mary Magdalene's, attention. 'Mother, this girl is very sick.'

Mother Mary Magdalane came over, but all she said was, 'Get on with your work.' I couldn't believe it! Then didn't the girl fall down beside me. The iron fell with her. Mother Mary Magdalene had left the room, so I shouted to another girl to get her back, and she went running off to look for the nun as I tried to help the girl. But I couldn't. Her whole body was twitching, her eyes were bulging and she was making this terrible choking noise. I shook her, but that did no good. I was crying because I couldn't help her, and as I watched she went blue and choked on her own tongue. She stopped breathing, and she died right there beside me. I stood there in despair.

'Sister. She's not breathing,' I sobbed, but Mother Mary Magdalene acted as if I had never even spoken. Taking the girl's wrist to check for life, she just nodded calmly to herself, then said, 'She's gone to God.'

I screamed. I had hoped I'd been just imagining that she was dead.

'Stop that noise, and get on with your ironing,' said Mother

Mary Magdalene. 'You're one worker down now, and we don't want you running behind.'

The incident was never mentioned again. I don't remember a funeral. We didn't even know where the girl got buried. That changed something in me. I knew that the nuns didn't care about me – or the other penitents. But they were working for God, and they weren't even sad when one of us died. Why should I work for such cruel nuns?

After a month they got so fed up with me that they sent me to Limerick, to the laundry attached to the orphanage where I had started out.

'Ah, here's the troublemaker,' the nuns said, warily, when I arrived. They knew my reputation, not just from the Mothers at the Magdalene laundries, but from my time at the Mount school.

'I'm not a troublemaker,' I said. 'I'm just very sick.'

'Oh, sick is it?'

'And if you don't let me out of here, I'm going to run away, or jump the wall.'

'Okay then. Go!'

Well that took me by surprise. The nun was muttering on, saying the laundry was better off without lazy girls like me, but I didn't care. All I could think was, I'm free! For the first time ever, I'm free.'

CHAPTER 34

NANCY

IT WAS ALL very well being free, but I walked out of that door with no money. After all those years of slaving for the nuns, after all that work I had done for them, I hadn't a halfpenny in my pocket. I had only the clothes on my back. I had an old frock that had belonged to somebody else and no coat. I hadn't a toothbrush or a piece of soap. I had nothing. I was on the streets with nowhere to go.

I wandered around for hours and hours. The city was so strange to me. I looked into the shop windows and marvelled at all the clothes. I pressed my nose up against the glass and peered into the cafes, jealously watching all the people drinking and eating without a care in the world. The smell of the food made my stomach ache with hunger. It got so bad that I went up to the nuns in the Mount school. I couldn't think of what else to do. There was a man sitting on the steps outside, eating a sandwich. He had this great big mug of tea.

'Who gave you that sandwich?' I asked. He was so busy eating, that he didn't answer, so I asked him again.

'It was the Sisters,' he said.

I knocked on the door, and Sister Maria answered. 'I'm so hungry,' I said. 'I don't feel well. Could you please give me a cup of tea?'

'Oh it's you,' she said. 'Go away. You were destructive. I hear you're gone from here. And you begged and begged to go. Off with you now.' She slammed the door in my face.

I sat on the step thinking, *What in the name of God am I going to do? I have no money, no food, nothing.*

Eventually I walked on. And didn't I meet a little boy who was carrying a sliced pan loaf in a brown paper bag.

'Hello,' I said. 'I wonder, would you give me a slice of your bread.' He gave me this look, and I said, 'Just a small bit. I'm so hungry.'

'I'm sorry,' he said. 'I can't. If I do, my mother will kill me.' He walked off, as I struggled back the tears. Then he stopped and turned. 'You know, I think I will give you some bread. Come on, take a piece.' Before he could change his mind, I took the crust. It tasted so good! I will never forget that boy. He was about 11.

'Thank you!' I said, my eyes welling up from his kindness. 'I hope you don't get into trouble.'

'I will tell my mother I was hungry and I ate a little bit.' He smiled at me, then turned and walked off. By this time it was getting dark, so I walked down to the Augustinian church. I had nowhere else to go, and I stayed inside all the evening. At that stage of my life, I did and didn't believe in God. I was angry with him; too angry to pray.

It was getting very late and I was worried I would be thrown out onto the street. I slipped into the confession box, thinking nobody will think of looking in here. I knelt down on the kneeler, but it was uncomfortable staying in that position for too long, and my legs started to cramp, so every now and then I would stand up and shake out my legs. After a while I saw this fellow walking up and down the aisle, looking around to see if anyone was there. He didn't see me, and he locked up the church.

I waited in there for another hour or two, just in case someone might come back. Then, when it got really late, I came out and lay down, stretched across one of the pews. That was much more comfortable, but I was freezing cold and afraid as well.

I woke up so many times during the night that when morning came I still felt bone tired. As soon as it was light I took myself back into the confession box. An hour or so later, I noticed a woman come in. She took off her coat, put on an overall, and started to brush the floor. I was trying to keep quiet, but I had a terrible tickle in my throat and I couldn't help coughing. The woman looked alarmed.

Opening the door of the confession box, she looked at me, from head to toe, and gave out a big sigh.

'There is no confession this early, love,' she said.

I blushed to my roots. 'Oh,' I said. 'I thought there was.' I'm sure she must have known I had slept in the church, but she didn't say.

'I'd go home now,' she said. 'Get yourself a bit of breakfast, and come back after Mass, at 11. The Father will hear your confession then.'

'Thank you.' How I wished I could do that. Instead I walked around with nowhere to go, my stomach rumbling with hunger until I could bear it no longer. I saw a restaurant with buns and cakes in the window. Noticing the ladies' toilet near the door, I slipped in and had a quick wash. I planned to ask for some food, but the waitresses didn't look very friendly. As I was standing there, a middle-aged couple stood and went up to the counter to pay. They were a few chips left on one of the plates, covered in tomato sauce. Quick as a flash, I grabbed two chips and turned for the door. Then I heard a shout.

'What do you think you're doing?' It was the elder of the two waitresses, and she ran across that restaurant and grabbed me by the arm. She shook my hand and knocked the chips onto the floor; then she pulled a chip out of my mouth and hauled me towards the door. 'Now get out! And don't let me see you around here again. You hear?' I felt utter despair.

Over the next few days, I walked around with nowhere to go. It was autumn. Some days were sunny, but others were cold and I'd jump up and down trying to get warm. Some people were kind. A man in one shop gave me a bun and a drink of water. I slept each night in a church, though not always the Augustinian church. But I was so tired after three nights with little sleep, and so hungry with days of next to nothing to eat, that in the end desperate I decided to try the convent again. With my stomach aching from hunger, and afraid of rejection, I climbed up the steps and knocked on the door.

As the door opened, I pleaded, 'Please will you give me a cup of tea, and maybe some food. I've had nothing to eat, and I feel so weak.'

It was Sister Maria. 'Perhaps I *can* give you some food,' she said. I was so grateful that I put out my hands and almost cried in relief, 'Thank you!' In eagerness, I expected food to just magically appear.

'Not so fast with your thanks,' she said, slapping my hands away. 'You're not getting something for nothing.'

'What do you mean?'

'I mean, my girl, that if you want food, you're just going to have to work for it. You can stay here again, but there's to be none of your tricks.'

'My tricks?'

'None of this "I'm too sick" or any of your other trouble-making ways come to that. You can help with all the uniforms for the school. I'll give you a week; you can have food and shelter but then, my girl, if there's any nonsense from you – any nonsense at all – you'll be getting your marching orders. Do you understand?'

'Yes Sister. Thank you Sister.'

I felt so miserable as she showed me to a little cell where I would sleep on my own.

'We don't want you mixing with the others, Bernadine,' the Sister said when she showed me my tiny quarters. 'We can't have you stirring up trouble, now, can we?'

I lay in bed that night, and wondered if I could ever live in the world. I'd dreamed of escape, but when it came, I didn't know what to do with it. Nobody cared about me, and I didn't think they ever would.

The food was as bad in that Magdalene laundry as it had been in the other ones. But at least it was food – if not, ever, quite enough. I pressed the uniforms, and worked alongside the other girls, but I didn't get to know them. I was lonely, and would liked to have joined them in the dormitory.

They didn't send me away after a week; I was there for about a month, but then I was called from my work and asked to go into the Mother Superior's office. I wondered what I was supposed to have done wrong this time. Three other girls were called up there with me.

'Stand up straight, all of you. And look smart for heaven's sake. Someone is coming to see you.' I wondered who that could be, but didn't like to ask. I thought maybe it was a doctor.

I hoped so, too, because after I still felt weak and ill from wandering the streets that week.

We heard people talking, and the sound of footsteps on the stairs, and a postulant came in with a great big man. He looked rough to me, and very stern.

'Well here they are,' said the nun. 'Take your pick.' We looked at each other, then lowered our eyes. Did he think we were a litter of puppies? I crossed my fingers and prayed that he would not pick me. But he did. Straight away. He just pointed at me and said, 'I'll take her.' It seemed to me that he didn't even look at the other girls. I think, now, that maybe it had all been planned. And that the other girls were there just to make it look better. I don't know.

'Off you go then, Bernadine,' said the nun. 'And make sure you do all that is asked of you.' Nodding miserably, I followed him down the stairs, and out of the door.

CHAPTER 35

NANCY

I DIDN'T TAKE anything with me, no change of clothes. Nothing. I had no possessions of my own.

If someone had told me even the day before that I would be rescued from the laundry and offered a fresh start, I would have been pleased. But as he brought me to his car I thought about making a run for it. He had a mean face, and the more I looked at him the more I thought, *I don't like the look of you. You frighten me.* But I got into the car beside him and he drove off, outside the town.

The minute we arrived he took me out and showed me the cows, the sows and the chickens. 'You're to look after them. You understand?' he said, and I nodded.

But I hadn't understood that I was to be his slave. I didn't realise that until the next day. I was mucking out the cow barn and he came and knocked me to the ground. 'You're doing that wrong,' he bellowed. 'Look at all that clean straw you're throwing out. Do you want to bankrupt me girl?'

A week later, telling me I was too slow at giving the pigs the leftovers, he belted me on the head with a hay fork and the blood spurted out. He said, 'I was dying to get an unwanted bastard like you; someone I could kick around.'

He would bring my food out to the cow house. I'd have potatoes with a bit of gravy on it, and maybe some bread. He'd say, 'Give what you don't eat to the chickens.'

One day he hit me so hard on my hand that I had to go to the hospital. The cut was infected; I think I had blood poisoning. The nurses were kind, but they didn't check out the farmer. And when I went back to him he made me work, even though my hand was still paining me.

After I'd been in hospital, the farmer tried to get money from the social services to pay for the work time I'd missed. But he couldn't prove that I existed. I didn't have a birth certificate or even a baptismal certificate. So he took me back to the nuns in Limerick, and they sent me to a Magdalene laundry in New Ross. 'Make sure you get her baptised,' he said. 'Then I'll have her back.'

When I had been with the farmer, sleeping in the barn alongside the cows, I used to remember that when Jesus was born and was lying in the manger, the breath of the cow kept him warm. That thought used to comfort me. But when the farmer noticed that I liked being close to the cows, he said, 'If you sleep long enough with the cows, you will end up turning into a cow.' That thought played on my mind, as I lay there, trying to sleep.

One day at Mass in New Ross, the priest was breaking the host and I got a terrible fear over me. I became convinced that I really *was* going to turn into a cow. I looked down at my brown dress and I started screaming. I don't know what had come over me, but once I started I couldn't stop. One of the sisters dragged me out of the church. Then she shook me. 'We'll have to send you to the asylum,' she said. That made me scream even more.

I was baptised there and I got my certificate, after which the farmer came to take me back to work for him. He said, 'Now I can get a medical card in your name.'

When I saw him again I didn't know what to think. I was fit to crack up. I knew it would be terrible being back at the farm, and it was. But at least I wasn't locked away anymore. When I was out in the fields I could look across and see the chickens. The cows kept me warm at night and the green fields would cheer me up a little bit. In the Magdalene laundries you saw nothing, only grey walls.

There was just one person who was kind to me, Mrs Shields, who I met when taking the cows to a field some way from the farmhouse. I said, 'Hello,' and she asked me if I would like a puppy. She gave me this beautiful little dog, like a little terrier.

I called him Shep. I fed him on scraps left out for the chickens, and on the separated milk that came back from the creamery in a barrel. He'd sleep in the barn with me at night. He was a comfort and I loved him so much.

When a calf is a few weeks old, he is taken away from his mother and you give him fresh milk. The first time I did that, the farmer showed me how to give the calf my finger so he knows to lick the milk. One day, when I was feeding the calf, it kicked out at the bucket and it banged into my shin. I screamed with the pain and let the bucket go. The milk spilt, and seeing that the farmer went for me like a lunatic. He tied me to a gate and forced spoonfuls of salt into my mouth. I couldn't breathe.

I shouted out, 'Help me! I'm going to die.' My face had gone all red, and my eyes were bulging. The farmer untied the ropes, and I ran for my life down to the end of the field. I was mad thirsty. I took a rusty old bean tin, filled it from the water pump and I drank and I drank. My stomach got bloated, and there were these splotches on my hands and face. I felt raging hot.

I didn't dare go back to the cow house, so I took shelter under a tree and drifted off to sleep. When I woke it was dark, and I went, slowly, back into the barn. And when I got to the place where I slept, I looked up and there was Shep, hanging. His little eyes were looking at me, and his tongue was hanging out. I gasped, and put my hand to my mouth. I thought, *I am going to be sick.*

The farmer must have been really angry with me to do that. I cried and cried. Shep hung there for four days. After that, the farmer took his little body down, and then he burned him. The smell was terrible. I was standing there, crying as he dug a hole and buried Shep's burned remains. Then I turned to go back to the barn. But he yanked my hair, and said, 'I'm not finished with you yet.'

Straight after that he brought me into another old house and said, 'Get in.'

He bolted the door and he had this huge knife in his hand. He is finally going to kill me, I thought. I looked over and saw a pig in the corner, which he tied up with a rope and dragged over. The pig was squealing, and was struggling to get away.

Handing me the rope, the farmer told me to hold on tight. Then he fetched this big basin. He cut the pig's throat right there in front of me before pushing me down on my knees. He handed me a spoon and told me to stir the blood. I was crying so much over the poor pig, but he was digging me in the back shouting, 'If you don't keep stirring that blood it will go into clots. And if that happens, I will kill you.'

I had nobody to turn to. Nobody. And I tell you this, if I knew what suicide was when I was with the farmer, I wouldn't be sitting here today. I would have been dead in the farmer's yard.

CHAPTER 36

NANCY

I HAD BEEN back with the farmer for three months or so, and each day seemed worse than the one before. The farmer was brutal. He was hitting me more and more.

Mrs Shields noticed I had some grey hair, and offered to take me to have it coloured. The farmer said hairdressers were not for the likes of me so he rubbed black shoe polish all over my hair. The small was terrible and my hair stuck together in a matted, tangled mess. 'That's better!' he said. 'You don't need hair colour now. Nobody will know whether you are grey or not.'

Soon after that, there was a terrible thunder storm in the night. I was terrified. And that was when I decided to run away.

I left the farmer that very day, as soon as the storm had cleared. The farmer had to take some pigs to the market, and the moment he drove away from the yard I made my escape.

A lorry stopped for me and took me to Limerick. I had nowhere to go. I was scared that if I went to the nuns, I would be sent back to the farmer again. They had never done anything for me except tell me I was a penitent and worth nothing. I looked terrible. Even worse than the last time I turned up on their doorstep. I was wearing a flour sack instead of clothes, and the polish was still in my hair.

So I decided to seek refuge in the churches again. The next day, when I was sheltering in St Joseph's Church, a lady approached and tapped me on the shoulder. 'Hello my dear,' she said. 'You don't look well love. Are you alright?'

Her hair was grey and she was wearing a navy blue coat. I looked down at my stiff sacking and felt ashamed. I wasn't used to hearing kind words, and I began to cry.

'I don't know what to do with myself,' I said. 'I don't feel well, and I'm tired. I have no money and no home. I don't have anywhere to go.'

'What's your name?' she asked.

'Nancy,' I said. It felt good to use that name. The name the woman in Adare had given me all those years before. I liked the name better than Kathleen, and much, much better than Bernadine.

'Where have you been living?'

I wouldn't tell her. I just began to cry harder.

She put an arm around me. 'Don't worry,' she said. 'You just come along with me.' She took me up to her house, ran a bath for me and found a frock for me to wear. She cooked me dinner, then drove me to a hostel in Limerick.

The warden in the hostel knew a married couple who needed someone to look after their children. She gave me the address, and pointed me towards the bus stop. I was very frightened on the bus by myself. I was shaking. But the wife met me off the bus, and took me to their house.

They had two little children, a boy called Tom and a girl

called Marina. They smiled at me shyly when we arrived, and followed me and their mother up the stairs as she showed me to my room.

Lying in bed that first night felt like heaven. I was about 22 years old. I was warm and safe, and finally living with a family who were nice to me. But I was terrified the farmer would come looking for me, and would drag me back to the barn.

I am embarrassed, now, when I think that I went into their house in such a state. The wife helped me to wash the polish out of my hair, but it took wash after wash. Then she got somebody in to put some colour in my hair. She got me some clothes as well.

The couple owned a shop in Limerick, and while they worked there they trusted me to stay home and look after their children. Three more followed over the years; their names are Alan, Leon and Cecil.

I had nothing when I came out of the laundry. Then the children came into my life. Since then they have been my life. I love them as if they were my own. I remember, when the children were small we watched television together. I loved that. Alan would love *Wanderly Wagon*, especially Ed the horse.

I'd tell the children stories at night. I'd use the stories I remembered from the Mount school, but I would change the endings. In my story, the three little pigs all lived happily ever after. When I looked at the children's little faces, I felt so happy; but I never lost the fear in me that I would be put back into the Magdalene laundry again.

As well as giving me a home, the family gave me money. I remember the first time I walked into a shop and bought buns. They tasted so good! It made up for the time when I was so hungry in Limerick and looked at the buns through the window. I bought sweets too. KitKat was my favourite. And I'd buy a packet of biscuits and share them with the children.

It took a long time before I knew that I didn't have to live the way I had lived in the laundry. When I got to know myself in the world, I got myself a set of false teeth which made me feel better.

I didn't get my social welfare for years. I tried, but the authorities were always asking about my birth certificate. The nuns didn't give me one and when I asked about it they said, 'You won't need one where you are going.'

All my life I have wanted to be a waitress. But I couldn't be one because I hadn't had an education. I wish I had stayed longer at school. I could read, but only write a little. I could write a card to the children and say, 'from Nancy', but I couldn't write well enough to say the things I wanted to. Recently, I have been going to classes to learn to write better.

I learned more from the children when they were growing up than I ever learned at the Mount school. They would learn their lessons and then would tell me the stuff. One time an aeroplane flew over the house. I said, 'What's an aeroplane in Irish?'

And Alan said, '*Eitléan*.'

After a few years I moved with the family to Galway, and I live with the couple there still. It's been good being part of a family. The children have all left home now, but they ring me every day and I see the ones who live nearby. I went to London to stay with Alan when he lived there, and since I got my birth certificate and my passport during the time of the Redress Board, I have been to Boston to stay with Cecil.

When I came out of the laundry I was always frightened. I would constantly look around me. And when I'd go to Mass I'd feel that the roof was going to fall in on top of me. I was just nervous. I often had to walk out because I was afraid, but over the years it went away.

I've never had a boyfriend. I could never meet anyone because I was always locked in. I was frightened of being shut away again, and my fear of the farmer had made me frightened of men. And I always had the children, who gave me all the love I needed.

I still have my good days and my bad days. I don't want to take my bitterness out on anyone so I keep my sadness inside me. I don't want to be uncharitable, but the nuns hadn't one bit of sympathy for me. Not ever. People say they were victims too. Some of the postulants were holy and were in the convent because they wanted to take vows, but others had been forced in. Yet they didn't have to be cruel. The nuns in Limerick were my family, but they sent me away.

The farmer tried to apologise to me. This was years later. I met his brother while I was out shopping while living with the family in Limerick. He said that the farmer had had a heart attack and was in hospital and that he wanted me to go out and see him so he could tell me he was sorry. Well, he had a lot to be sorry for. I did go, but when I walked into the ward his new wife took one look at me and chased me out into the corridor.

Some years later people started talking about the abuse in orphanages. You could get money to make up for the way the nuns treated you there. I applied and I got some money. Then people started saying the Magdalene women should get some money too.

I watched Enda Kenny apologise on television. I saw all the women cheering and crying at the same time. Afterwards I went to my solicitor to see if I could get compensation. He said that I would not be able to because I had the money for being in an orphanage. But his secretary didn't agree with him. She said maybe it was worth a try and she gave me Steven O'Riordan's number. I went home, picked up the phone and dialled.

CHAPTER 37

NANCY

THE DAY I told Steven my story, I was bawling crying on the phone and he was kind. He said, if I could get to Dublin, I could meet other women from the laundries and could tell my story to a judge called Justice Quirke. Then I could, maybe, get compensation.

I didn't know how I would get to Dublin, but Alan said he would drive me there in his taxi. Then Leon said he would come too. He could see I was frightened. They were very good. They weren't allowed to go with me into the court, but they waited for me. They were a great support.

The court was in a building called the Commissions Office. I walked in and met Steven. There were lots of other women there, asking me questions like 'Were you in the Good Shepherds?' I listened to them but I didn't talk. I felt lost.

We waited to see the judge for a long time and Steven went to complain. It was getting late, and some of the women were worried that they might not catch their train home. I worried too. Alan had to get back to Galway with his taxi.

'And, as you need to get home, you can go in the first group. Is that okay, Nancy?' he asked.

I was shaking. 'I don't want to be going first,' I said. 'I don't want everybody to hear my story. I don't want anyone to know what happened to me.'

'Then you can go last in the group,' he said. 'We'll tell the judge.'

I felt strange going into the room. There was a round table at which the judge sat. He said, 'Good afternoon, ladies. Thank you so much for coming all this way. I'm Justice Quirke, and I want to hear your stories.'

I sat down first. I sat on the chair to the right of the judge. I did that so that I could tell my story last. But he turned to me and said, 'We'll start to my right and go round the room.'

'No!' I said. 'Could we start from your left?'

Then Steven said, 'Nancy doesn't want to tell her story in public. She would prefer to tell you in private.'

But all the women were saying, 'Ah Nancy! You go first. You tell your story, it will be fine.'

So I said, 'Alright then. I'll go. I'll tell my story.'

'Are you sure now?' asked Steven.

'I can't tell it very well,' I said, 'but I'll tell it the best I can.'

The room was quiet. I told about the grotto and the swing, and the laundry. Some of the women were nodding and saying, 'I remember that too.' When I got to the bit about the girl breaking her neck, I could hear sniffles around me. Everyone was staring at me. I think they were emotional.

I cried and cried when I got to the bit about the farmer killing my dog. Then I said, 'That's my story.'

There was silence. Then Steven said, 'Ah Nancy, give them a happy ending!'

'Have I time? Surely someone else should go now?'

But the judge spoke for the first time. He was so kind. He said, 'No, no. Take your time.' So I said about the woman in the church, and about the family.

The judge said he would take a short break because so many people were crying. Nobody moved for a while. Then the women came up to me and said, 'Nancy, that is the worst story I have ever heard.' They said it was much worse than theirs. They said they couldn't believe it. They said I was amazing! Even Steven looked shocked, and he had heard so many stories, I'd say.

Now I had some support. I was never able to talk before, and it was always like there was a heavy weight on me. And some days you would say to yourself, 'If it weren't for the family you wouldn't care if you never got up.'

I remember one woman in particular from that day. It was Diane Croghan. She came up to me before I left and she put her arms around me. 'What you have been through, Nancy!' she said. 'How could anyone do that?' She was crying, and it was all for me.

CHAPTER 38

DIANE

I DON'T REMEMBER my mother, at least not from when I was a child. I was born in the county home in Enniscorthy in 1940. My mother chose my name, Diane, and she looked after me for a while. I know she did, because I have a photograph of her holding me in her arms. She looks happy. But she ran away and abandoned me when I was two years old. She was 18 then, and was just 16 when I was born. But I can never forgive her for leaving me there. For leaving her own child.

My records show that I stayed at the county home for another year. When I was three years old I was fostered out to Mr and Mrs Jordan in Kiltealy, a village not far from Enniscorthy. And I was happy enough there. Mrs Jordon was a bit strict; she used to hit me every now and again. She would lift my dress and slap me, hard, across the back of my legs. It hurt and I'd cry, but I'm sure I deserved it.

I liked Mr Jordon, which is more than Mrs Jordan did. She was terrible to him, treating him like a dog. He had once worked on a farm, but he was retired now so was in the house a lot. Mrs Jordan hated that.

'You're always under my feet,' she would say, hitting his legs with the sweeping brush as he sat on a chair by the range. He'd sit there to eat his dinner too, rather than at the table with us. I don't know why. He rarely had the same dinner as us. He was happy with just a mug of goodey – that's bread soaked in a cup of tea.

Every Friday he would walk the three miles to the village to collect his pension. That was hard for him, because he walked with two sticks. When he'd collected his money, he would cross over to the school gate and call out to me. I'd run over, and he'd put tuppence in my hand.

'That's to spend on sweets,' he'd say. That was worth a good few bob in those days. He called me his Dinah, and the name stuck.

Mrs Jordan liked to invite the neighbours in for a game of whist. They'd sit round the table, playing and talking, but Mr Jordon never joined in. It was like he wasn't there. I would be sitting at the table with Rita, my foster sister who was six years older than me, listening to the conversation. One day I heard the neighbours talking about the Black and Tans. They had shot Mr Jordan in the knees. That's why he was lame. I wondered what the Black and Tans were, and I asked my teacher at school the next day.

'The bloody English. Enemies of the state,' was all he would say.

Sometimes they would be talking about a husband's drinking or someone owing lots of money from betting on horses. I tried to be invisible, because if they noticed me sitting, wide-eyed as I listened, they would change the subject and send me to bed. There was no electricity in the cottage. I'd light a gas lamp, take it upstairs with me and blow it out once I was in bed. Sometimes the shadows on the wall scared me.

Mrs Jordan slept in a room with Rita, and I slept in the same room as Mr Jordan – in the same bed. I never thought that odd at the time, though looking back I can see it was strange. I am almost certain that no abuse happened, but there was one thing I really hated. Mr Jordan had a bad chest. He would cough up a lot of thick phlegm and smear it over the blankets. I don't remember the blankets ever being washed, so the smell lingered. It made me retch.

The Jordans had a third foster daughter called Betty, but she was even older than Rita and by the time I was at school she was working away in Dublin. She came to visit sometimes. She'd sit with Mrs Jordan telling all her stories about the city, and Mrs Jordan would laugh. The house always seemed brighter and more full of life when she was around.

One time, though, when she came down from Dublin, Mr Jordan was lying sick in the bed. He spent quite a lot of time in bed. She went up to see him and he made some comment about the way she was dressed. She didn't say a word, but she kicked him, hard. I thought that was terrible. I was waiting for Mrs Jordan to scold her, but she didn't say a word. It was like she just didn't care.

We didn't go hungry. We would eat potatoes and cabbage, and occasionally we'd have chicken as the Jordan's kept some hens in a run in the garden. I hated watching Mrs Jordan twist the chicken's neck to kill it, especially as it seemed to give her pleasure. She'd get me or Rita to pluck the bird, and clean out its guts ready to be boiled in water. I hated that job.

I went to the national school in Kiltealy, but I didn't learn an awful lot there. When I left I couldn't read and write properly, and my maths wasn't up to much. That's because all the lessons were taught in Irish, even though it was not an Irish-speaking area and we didn't speak it in the house. I can count up to 100 in Irish okay, and I still remember how to say, '*An bhfuil cead agam dul go dtí an leithreas*,' which means 'Can I go to the toilet?', and '*Suí síos agus ní bheidh ag caint*,' which translates as 'sit down and don't be talking'. But that doesn't get you very far in life.

The other problem was that I was left-handed. And left-handed people were considered evil. The teacher, Mr Powel, was always picking on me. One time, I went up to the blackboard to write a sum and I picked the chalk up with my left hand. Mr Powel whacked me across the knuckles and said, 'How many times do you have to be told? Don't use that hand!'

That wasn't the only time I felt his anger. When I got my sums wrong, or couldn't say my tables, he'd beat me with a leather strap. 'If you can't do better than this, you can go back to the county home you came from,' he'd say, as he lashed me on the hand. 'Back with all the other bastards.'

It was a terrible thing to be illegitimate. Mr Powel was always respectful to the farmer's daughters, but he took it out on me. The worst thing was that the other children picked it up from him. We'd be in the playground, and they'd come up to me and say, 'Where's your mammy Dinah? Where's your daddy?'

I'd just look at them confused, and they'd say, 'Oh Dinah, I forgot. You don't have any. You're a bastard.'

I used to lash out at them until I realised that it only got me into worse trouble, and then I learned to just ignore them.

If my friend Sadie Tobin went home and told her family she'd been playing with Dinah Hogan there'd be all hell to pay.

It wasn't so bad for Peggy and Nancy Cullen, because their parents didn't have any airs and graces. They lived in a council house.

On the way to school I passed an orchard. I watched the apples ripen, and one day on the way home, checking that nobody was watching me, I went in to rob some. I got a good few, and I had them gathered in my skirt. I was walking up these kind of wooden steps and didn't Mr Powel catch me. The next day he called me to the front of the classroom. He told everyone I had robbed apples, then gave me 10 of the best; five on each hand with a stick.

'Now don't let me catch anyone else robbing,' he said, as I rubbed my hand and tried not to cry.

I had a bad time at school, but it was worse still for some of the boys. They were always getting lashed for some minor misdemeanour. One of them, Philip, had such a terrible time that he cut off his own thumb so that he would not have to go back. That shocked us all so much.

When it came to our Holy Communion we had to learn the catechism. That didn't worry me, but what did was that I had to have a white dress, and I was too scared to ask Mrs Jordan to pay for one. There was a lot of talk at school about it. Then one day when I got home from school there was a big parcel with my name on it. I opened it, carefully cutting the string and ripping the tape, and inside was this white dress all wrapped up in tissue paper.

I pulled the dress out, and stared at it in wonder. It was the most beautiful thing I had ever seen. It had a flower on it, and coloured ribbons flowing from the flower. I gasped with happiness. 'Thank you Mrs Jordan,' I said.

'Don't thank me,' she said, in her usual off-hand way. 'You

don't really think that I'd spend that kind of money for a dress you'd wear just once do you?'

'Then where did it come from?'

'It was your mother sent it,' she said.

'My mother?' Just the mention of her made me tremble. Did that mean my mam had *not* completely abandoned me? Did she, maybe, think of me sometimes? I let myself dream and imagined she would be coming to the ceremony. I didn't ask the Jordans if she would be there. I just waited, breathless, for the day to come.

There we all were, lined up in the church. I kept turning round scanning the pews, looking at all the other mothers. I got a clatter for fidgeting. And of course she never came. I was to wait many, many years before I caught sight of her.

One thing that I was good at was singing. I remember the priest, Father Redmond, called at the house one day, and asked the Jordans if they could spare me for his church choir. 'Dinah has the voice of an angel,' he said. I loved that, and looked forwards to all the rehearsals. At Christmas I was chosen to sing a solo. It was 'Adeste Fideles'.

The church was full for that service, and it looked beautiful bathed in candle light. There was a hush as I started to sing. As my voice drifted up into the rafters, everyone was listening, just to me. That gave me the biggest thrill.

Mrs Jordan had occasional work on a farm and sometimes she would take me with her. I'd wash potatoes ready for thrashing. Sometimes I'd get paid. I loved having a shilling to spend on sweets.

A while after my first communion, Mr Jordon began to spend more and more time in bed. The doctor came to the house to see him. When he came downstairs again, Mrs Jordan asked how her husband was, and he said, 'Oh, he's all bound up. You'd need a chisel and hammer to move him.'

I didn't understand what he meant, until later I overheard Mrs Jordan telling a neighbour, over a cup of tea. 'It's his bowels,' she was saying. 'There's a blockage, and he's all bunged up.'

One day when I came home from school Mr Jordan wasn't there. He'd been carted off to the hospital. I never saw him again.

The atmosphere in the house changed and I spent as long out of it as I could. I'd hang around the street, talking to friends, laughing and watching the boys playing football. I always seemed to be in trouble. I'd hear Mrs Jordan and a neighbour talking about me. 'She's wild that one,' she'd say. 'The boys will have an eye for her soon, her and her curls, and then there will be trouble.'

'Ah sure, she'll end up like her mother, so she will.'

Sometime after that, Father Redmond turned up at as I was eating my breakfast.

'Hello Dinah,' he said. 'I've come to take you on a trip.'

'Why?' I looked at Mrs Jordan, but she didn't catch my eye.

'You're a lucky girl. You're not going to school today,' he said.

'Why not?' I replied, confused at this sudden change in plan.

'You're coming with me.'

'But where are we going?'

'You'll see,' he said. And I followed him out of the door.

CHAPTER 39

DIANE

I THOUGHT, PERHAPS, Father Redmond was taking me to the church. It was coming up to Easter and, maybe, I was needed for a choir practise. But he drove past the church, and out into the countryside. Then we arrived at this massive building, with a door fit for a giant.

'Here we are Dinah,' he said. 'This is Summerhill training school for girls.'

I was trembling when he pulled that bell. A nun answered, and led us into a hallway. There were holy statues everywhere you looked. Then we were taken into this parlour, and were left sitting at this beautiful mahogany table. It was so shiny I could see my face reflected in it. The chairs around it matched. When I sat down beside Father Redmond I almost slipped off.

'Stop fidgeting,' he said, as I tried to settle myself better in the chair.

'You're to be good, Dinah, do you hear?' he said. 'I don't want to hear any reports about bad behaviour, you understand?'

'Am I going home Father?'

'I'll be back for you,' he said, but he didn't look at me as he said it.

'Okay, Father.' I was puzzled. 'When?'

'Soon. And meanwhile the nuns will take care of you. You're lucky. They are wonderful, dedicated people. You will be taught how to get on in the world. It will be the making of you.'

'Don't leave me,' I pleaded, tears threatening to come. 'Take me home. I'll be good. I promise. I will be.'

Just then this nun swept into the room, and stared at me. Then, greeting Father Redmond, she said, 'This is the girl is it?'

I was pleased that she spoke in English and not Irish. Maybe, now, I would learn to read and write.

'She's not very big, is she?'

'But she's strong, Sister Bernadette,' said Father Redmond. 'And she's able. Her foster mother has trained her well.'

'Come with me and we'll get you changed,' said Sister Bernadette, sweeping me out of the room. Father Redmond didn't say goodbye. And I never saw him again.

Before I knew it, I was out of my clothes and into this horrible grey tunic thing made of calico – which was shapeless, like a kimono. Taking my beautiful hornpipe shoes away, Sister Bernadette handed me these battered lace up brogues that pinched my toes. 'You'll need this too,' she said, handing me a kind of bib to wear over the top of the dress. Then she approached me with these shears, and laid into my hair. I looked at the floor, where my ringlets lay abandoned, and felt like crying.

'That's better,' said Sister Bernadette, looking at my jagged pudding basin. 'Now you're ready for life here. And I hope Father Redmond is right, Dinah. Are you a hard worker?'

'Yes Sister,' I said, doubtful that my old teacher would agree. But now that I was 12, I thought it was time to get down to learning to read and write well. I didn't realise that I was here to do the work of an adult, but I found out soon enough. To the outside world, Summerhill was a training school for young women. But it was actually a Magdalene laundry run by the Sisters of Mercy. There was absolutely nothing merciful about those nuns – I might as well have been thrown into prison.

The first few days were confusing to me. It's like you've been totally disowned. Nobody wants you, you're in this strange place where you can't talk, and you can't have food when you want it. You just take what you are given.

The days took on a punishing routine. Get up, kneel by the bed for a morning prayer; wash and dress, making sure to keep your nightdress on until all your clothes were on; go to chapel for Mass; eat a breakfast of bread and butter, or once in a while a kind of yellow porridge called stir-about. Clean the convent, scrubbing corridors on our hands and knees; go to the laundry. Slave there all day in silence. Then it was dinner of cabbage and potato, or maybe a watery stew, and back to chapel for more praying.

The work was terribly hard. I was put on the calendar, this terrible roller thing, and we had to feed in sheets. Some of us smaller ones had to stand on a wooden platform to reach it. It was hard feeding in the sheets as the roller was steaming hot.

The hardest thing of all was keeping the sheets straight. That was tricky for everyone, but especially for me. I was left-handed, and the nuns hated that as much as Mr Powel at the school had. A Sister – I don't remember her name so we'll call her Ursula – was in charge. She had her pets among the girls, but I was not one of them. And she would make me go on the right-hand side of the calendar to make life as hard for me as she could. The girl on the other side was a bully. If the sheets weren't in straight, as often they weren't, she'd call over Sister

Ursula and tell on me and I'd get a sharp whack on the back of my hand. One day Sister hit me so hard that my hand split open.

I was crying in pain, but all Sister cared about was the blood pouring onto the sheet.

'Look at that, you dirty girl,' she said, whisking me away to the kitchen, where she got some salt and poured it on the wound. I can still remember the pain of it. They didn't call a doctor or even give me a bandage, and the cut gaped for a while. I still have the scar to this day.

CHAPTER 40

DIANE

WHEN I WASN'T crying in pain, I was crying inside. I cried for my friends, for Mr Jordan, and for the life I had known. God knows it had not been perfect, but I had been free. Here we lived in fear. We walked around with our heads bowed. I became quiet and withdrawn, and that's not like me.

We slept in huge dormitories with 20 beds in each, and even at night we couldn't talk. There was a large internal window and behind it was a room where a nun sat. It seemed to me that she never ever slept. If we so much as whispered she'd appear, and shove us out onto the balcony for a while to teach us a lesson.

The biggest sin of all was wetting the bed. I never did that, but a couple of girls did. There would be a bed inspection in the morning, and if the nuns found wet sheets they would strip them off the beds and tie them around the girl's faces.

They'd do the same if there was blood on the bed when you had your period. But as they limited the number of horrible, bleached-cloth sanitary towels we were allowed, that was almost impossible to prevent. I got caught that way more than once.

They never called us by our names in that place. Sometimes they used our numbers; I was number 83, but usually it was just a pointed finger and, 'You! And you, and you!'

If the work was hard – and it was child slavery – the conditions, with the steam, heat and constant whining of the machines, made it unbearable. I could, maybe, have borne that, but never to get outside the door? Never to have a normal conversation, that was what broke me. I'd gone from a country home where I had people I thought of as a family, where I had friends. All that had been taken away from me when I was put in there.

When I'd been there a week, I asked if I could write to Mrs Jordan. You'd think I'd asked for the sun, moon and stars for the fuss that was made.

'No, Diane, you may not!' said Sister Ursula, turning on her heel. She never gave me a reason, but I know the nuns were scared I'd tell Mrs Jordan how miserable I was. We weren't allowed to receive letters either. Not one. And I never, ever had a visitor. I might as well have died for all my friends on the outside knew.

Once a week, on Saturdays, we queued up to wash our hair. There was always a scramble to get to the front, and I never managed it. There were two older nasty girls, who would elbow you in the ribs and force their way to the head of the queue. Because I was small and quiet, I was easy to push around. By the time I reached the top of the queue and had my head pushed down in the deep basin, the water would be cold. And that wasn't the worst of it. It would be covered in scum, too, and there would be lice floating on the top.

And woe betide you if you were the one to have lice! You'd

be dragged off roughly and have your hair chopped off. One girl had such bad lice, and she scratched so much, that she ended up with scabs all over her scalp. The nuns hacked her hair to the bone, leaving her with unsightly cuts. They were so cruel.

After washing our hair we had to line up wearing nothing but our knickers. Then the nuns would go along the row examining us to see if we were clean. To us adolescents, who were normally forced to hide our embarrassingly developing bodies, that exposure was excruciating!

All of this was done so that we would look nice for Mass on Sundays; the nuns were always telling us that we had to show respect to God. Funny that. We went to Mass every day of the week, and they didn't care how we looked from Monday to Saturday.

We didn't work on Sundays – but only because it's a sin to work on the Sabbath. In the afternoons we were taken out, around the town. When I heard we were going walking that first Sunday, I was so excited to be seeing the outside world again. But the nuns made sure we didn't enjoy ourselves.

We had to walk in a crocodile, two by two, as if we were animals lining up to go into Noah's Ark. The nuns came with us to make sure that we didn't talk. It was demeaning. I remember seeing families walking around, laughing together, and I wondered if I would ever, in my life, be part of a family again. Would I ever be anything other than miserable? I *hated* those walks. I hated the way everyone would stare at us as if we were freaks. If you stared back they couldn't get away fast enough.

On our way out we passed this big door. There was a rumour that behind the door there was a corridor that led to the neighbouring St Peter's College. That was a school run by priests. It was very posh and was for boys of rich families. That door fascinated us. And when, during the week, we'd be shoved into the yard to get some fresh air, we'd try turning the handle. It was always locked, but we lived in hope. If we got through it perhaps one of the boys would help us to get out of the place. I used to fantasise about that. I'd imagine that a boy would think I was the prettiest girl he had ever seen. He would take me home to his family and they would let me stay. Then I'd put my hand to my head, feel my jagged shorn hair and realise I was now as ugly as sin.

I was *always* dreaming of getting out of there. I'd think about it during Mass, during meals and during work. But most of all in those endless hours when we lay in bed. I didn't get as far as planning my escape, but one day I was in the hall, waiting to see Sister Bernadette. When Sister Bernadette answered the phone she would say, 'Are you still there?' Except the way she said it, the word came out as 'sshtill'. I was laughing about that as I waited.

She was about to call me into her office when the doorbell rang. She opened it, let in the priest, then shut the door again. She took out her key to lock the door when the telephone rang. She rushed across, and picked up the receiver. Her back was turned and, seizing my chance, I slipped out of the door. I remember breathing in, tasting freedom!

I ran as fast as I could, but I had no idea where I was headed. I didn't care, just as long as it was away from that prison; away from the torture. I reached the edge of Wexford Town, and, out of breath, I stopped running. But just as I thought I was safe, a hand landed on my shoulder. I looked round and saw a Garda.

'Thought you'd get away, did you,' he said, leading me to a Garda car which had stopped a few yards behind me. 'Are you going to be a good girl and come quietly, or do I need the handcuffs?' He rattled them in my face and I recoiled. I sat quietly in the back of the car, terrified of what would happen to me now. As well I might be.

Sister Bernadette answered the door, as I knew she would, and her face was puce with anger. 'How *dare* you run out on me like that,' she said, and pulled me roughly down a corridor. 'Will someone come and help me with this tearaway?'

Two older girls appeared, and they held me down. I thought, it had to be them; the bossiest, nastiest girls in the place. And Sister Bernadette came at me with a pair of scissors. I was used to having my hair chopped by Sister Bernadette. She's get the clippers out the moment a curl dared to appear, but this time she really meant business. Hacking my hair down to the scalp, she said, 'This will teach you. You won't go trying to escape again now, will you?'

I was screaming and kicking out, and the more I kicked, the harder the girls gripped my arms. When my hair had been mutilated to Sister Bernadette's satisfaction, one of them pushed me away so roughly that I was catapulted across the room. Then she called me back and told me to sweep up my hair. As a final insult, she came at me with a mirror, and made me look in it – the only time in that place I ever saw one. 'Not so pretty now, are you,' she sneered. 'And now for your punishment.'

And I thought, *Isn't making me look like a monster punishment enough?*

'Off to the laundry with you,' she said. She had me on my hands and knees buffing that whole big room. It took me hours and hours. I was sobbing, quietly. It wasn't the punishment so much that hurt – well, it did, but I was crying more because I had so nearly got away. I thought, if only I had taken a different road. If only the Garda hadn't seen me. If only.

Just as I was finishing my punishment one of the younger

nuns came into the room. I cowered, expecting a beating, but she put her hand on my jagged head, gently. 'Don't do that again,' she said. 'You've nobody to run to, and you'll never get far. And believe me, there's much, much worse they can do to you than cut your hair.'

I looked at her in surprise. What could possibly be worse than that? But I appreciated her trying to comfort me. It was rare enough to get kind words in that hellish place.

I wondered if those horrible girls would end up staying on, and become like Mollie Doyle, a woman who caused us no end of grief. She was taken into the convent as a child; she had stayed, and now had her own room. She would take us there and give us a right old walloping. Even the nuns were frightened of Mollie Doyle.

'She was worse than the nuns,' said Mary, a woman from Wexford who came to see me one time. 'She'd take us into her room and give us a right old beating. She hit us and taunted us, and always found fault with our work. Even the nuns were frightened of Mollie.'

For all the cruelty of the Sisters of Mercy, religion was important to me. I never stopped believing in God; not for a single moment. I always knew he would look after me, and that's how I got through.

We were all so excited when one of the nicer nuns, Sister Patricia, was professed and took her final vows. We were all herded up to the balcony at the back of the church to watch. It was just like a wedding, and Sister Patricia was the bride. She was all dressed in white, and looked so beautiful, but instead of kissing her groom, she had to lie down with her arms out and prostate herself to God, then kiss the floor. We thought it was wonderful!

Days leaked into weeks, and the months turned into years.

I'm not sure exactly how long I was in the laundry, because the nuns didn't keep accurate records, but what I *do* know for sure is that freedom was just around the corner.

CHAPTER 41

DIANE

I WASN'T LET out of the laundry. Sometimes I really wonder if I ever would have been if I hadn't taken my chance at escape – because escape I did! I was 15 years old. This time I planned it carefully. I was set to work in the packing room, with another girl, Mary. We weren't friends exactly – it was hard to get close to anyone when you weren't allowed to open your mouth – but we were both desperate to get out of that laundry.

Every day the vans would come in through the back entrance of the convent with bags of dirty sheets collected from the hotels in the area. We would help unload the van and then load it again with bags of clean laundry. Sister Ursula would supervise us and take care of all the paperwork.

One day, having loaded the van, we hung around behind it out of sight. The van driver called over Sister Ursula, asking her to sign all the forms. And when they were deep in conversation we hopped into the back of the van, and hid behind the laundry bags. Sister Ursula assumed we had gone back into the laundry, as usual, and the van driver just shut the back door without a thought.

I hardly dared breathe for excitement. And when the van pulled up to Whites hotel in Wexford to deliver the clean laundry, he took the first load in and left the back of the van open. We looked at each other, then hopped out and legged it. Mary went in one direction, and I went in another.

The next thing I knew I was in Dublin's most famous street, O'Connell Street. I know *now* that I was in O'Connell Street – the place where the Easter Rising of 1916 started – but I didn't know that then. I hadn't a clue where I was.

The odd thing is, to this day, I don't know how I got from Whites hotel to Dublin. It's like I landed there from nowhere. As if I was dropped from the sky.

That lapse of memory has always bothered me. But recently, when I saw a psychologist for counselling, he asked me how I had got out of the laundry. And I said, 'I hitched a lift on a laundry van.'

'And then?'

I shrugged. 'I don't know. I remember the van as if it was yesterday. I remember the thrill of freedom, and I remember shouting "good luck" to Mary as we ran off. But I haven't a breeze what happened next, or how I got to Dublin.'

He looked at me for a while. He tapped his pen on the desk, then he said, 'You wouldn't want to remember, Diane.'

I couldn't think what he meant. 'Yes I do,' I said. 'It's been bothering me for years.' He shook his head at me, his gaze serious.

'You think I'm making myself forget on purpose?'

He nodded, and looked at me, over the top of his glasses. 'I'd say you've blanked it out, because you can't bear to remember.'

We sat in silence. Then I said, 'So something really awful happened to me?'

'Perhaps.'

'Was I with a man?'

He shrugged his shoulders, but I know now that is what he meant. Maybe I was attacked? I would have been in clothes from the laundry, and girls from a laundry were thought to be fallen women. People called us prostitutes. We had no money, no belongings. Nobody who wanted us. So of *course* nobody respected us. We were easy prey.

I shivered at the thought. Because if I *had* been with a man, he'd scarpered by the time we reached Dublin. So obviously, whatever he did, or I did, I had blanked it out. I've tried, again, to piece it all together, but I just can't remember.

I *do* remember my first sight of that wide street. I remember the statue of Nelson, the one that later got blown up by the IRA. I remember my first sight of Clerys department store, and that clock that hangs outside, where everyone meets. It looked so grand to me; I had seen nothing like it in my whole life. I remember looking in the window, wishing I had money and could buy the fancy fur coat displayed there. It was a warm day for January, but even so I shivered with the cold.

I remember wandering up the street, slowly, mesmerised by all the buses, and all the people hopping on and off them without a care in the world. And I thought that all this life had been going on, all the time, and there I had been slaving away for the nuns. It didn't seem possible.

I didn't know what to do. Then I noticed this man standing at the bottom of some steps wearing a top hat, and a fancy coat with tails and brass buttons. He was helping a woman into a taxi, and I thought maybe he would be able to help me too. So

I walked up to him, and stood there, in front of him.

'Yes?'

'Could you please tell me where I am?' I asked.

'O'Connell Street, Dublin,' he said. 'And where is it you want to go?'

'I'm not sure,' I said. 'I'm just up from the country, and I'm on the lookout for a job.'

'Are you now?' He looked me up and down, and I thought, *Ah no, he's going to send me back to the laundry*. I started to shake, but he smiled, kindly. 'And have you anywhere to stay while you look?' he asked.

I shook my head, and waited for trouble. But it didn't come. 'There's a hostel just up the road there,' he said. 'In Parnell Square.' Then, winking, he handed me five shillings. 'Tell them the concierge at the Gresham Hotel sent you.'

'Oh thank you!' I said, and ran up the road before he could change his mind and ask for his money back. But that wonderful man hadn't finished with me. Three days later he appeared at the hostel and asked me if I had found a job. And of course, I hadn't.

He nodded to this woman who was standing behind him, and she stepped forwards and shook my hand. 'Hello, I'm Mrs Everall.' She was wearing a beautifully cut camel coat.

'I'm Diane,' I said, deciding there and then that I didn't want to be called Dinah ever again. It was too childish for me, now that I was to live in Dublin City.

'Can you cook?' she asked, and I nodded, even though the only experience I had was helping Mrs Jordan back in the day.

'Do you like children?'

'Oh yes! I love them.'

She smiled at my enthusiasm. 'Good. I think you will make a perfect housekeeper. Would you like to work for me?'

'Oh yes! Yes please,' I said.

She laughed. 'My husband and I both work, and we have two children. Boys. They're young still – one is four, the other 18 months, so they don't go to school yet. Does that sound okay?'

'Oh yes!' And it did.

The Everalls lived nearby in Donnybrook, a smart place on the outskirts of Dublin city centre. Mr Everall was a lecturer in Trinity College, Dublin's most historic university. Before I saw the house, Mrs Everall took me to a small clinic or hospital. I was put in a cubicle and told to take my clothes off. Then I was checked over – first by a nurse, then by a doctor.

They looked into my throat and my ears, and shone a light into my eyes. They listened to my chest and made me breathe in and out. They examined my limbs; they asked me how I got my scar, and I was vague and just said I'd cut it. There was no way I was going to tell them the truth – that a nun had hurt me in a Magdalene laundry. I had never in my life been examined so thoroughly. And I probably never have been since! Then, putting on rubber gloves, the nurse picked through my hair. She pursed her mouth, as if she was sucking lemons. It made me feel very dirty, but then I was!

When I had dressed again, they took me out to reception. And to my relief, Mrs Everall was still there, flicking through a magazine. 'Well, she's in perfect health!' said the nurse. But then, muttering, she handed Mrs Everall a brown paper bag with a bottle inside. And the minute we arrived in Donnybrook, before I'd set eyes on the boys, she handed over the bottle, took me into a bathroom and told me to drench my hair with the liquid.

'If you leave this on overnight, we can use a fine comb on it in the morning,' she said, and I blushed. The liquid smelt disgusting. But it did the trick. I'd said goodbye to lice once and for all. I was clean. And most importantly, free.

CHAPTER 42

DIANE

THE NEXT DAY Mrs Everall knocked on my door and came in carrying some clothes. 'Here are some things I don't wear anymore, Diane,' she said. 'I think you're the same size as me.' There were some day dresses, and skirts and blouses. She waved away my thanks and said, 'It's nothing. Just a few bits to keep you going until you get some things of your own.'

Dressed, I went downstairs and found Mrs Everall in the kitchen with two very small boys. 'There you are,' she said. 'Meet Simon and Erik.'

'Hello!' I kneeled down to talk to them. The eldest, Simon, looked at me solemnly, but his brother, sitting in a high chair, was full of chat.

Before she left for work, Mrs Everall opened a cupboard and showed me the mops, dusters and polish. Then, opening the fridge, she told me to cook sausages for dinner, for myself and the boys.

I'd never seen a sausage so I hadn't a clue how to cook one, but I wasn't going to tell my employer that. So I said, 'How do the boys like their sausages cooked?' and she said, 'They like them fried in this pan.'

'And how do they like their potatoes cooked?'

'Here's the potato peeler,' she said, opening a drawer. 'Boil them for 20 minutes or so, and when they're soft you can mash them with some butter and milk. Is that okay?'

'Fine.'

Every day it was the same. I said, 'How do they like their fish cooked?' or their beans, or stews. I don't suppose Mrs Everall was fooled for one minute, but she let me keep my dignity. Very soon I got the knack of cooking, making chicken, fish and stews, and I found that I liked it very much indeed.

They were lovely little boys. I got on with them well, and had little trouble from them. When I was polishing the floor, they'd sit on my back and we'd pretend I was a horse. They loved that.

I worked hard at that job; but it was nothing compared to the laundry. I had a day off every Tuesday, and a half day on Thursday. I was free on every second Sunday too. I earned 25 shillings a week. Having slaved for nothing for years that seemed like riches!

There were some recipe books in the kitchen. I used to flick through the pages and look at the pictures, but I couldn't read the text. That really bothered me, and I decided I had to know how to read so that I could get on in life. It was one way to get back at the nuns who had always been telling me that I would amount to nothing.

I bought the *Dandy* and the *Beano* comics every week. I'd look at the cartoon pictures of Denis the Menace, Desperate Dan, the Bash Street Kids and Beryl the Peril, and I would break the words down into sounds. Slowly, but surely, the words began to make sense.

The Everalls were so good to me. When I'd been there about

a year, they sent me to a school of domestic economy, near their house in Donnybrook; this was on Thursday afternoons – my half day. I learned so many useful things there, like how to cook on a budget, and how to use leftovers.

After two years there, I heard of another, better paid job in housekeeping. I went for an interview, and was interested the moment I saw 'Moorings', the beautiful big house on Merrion Row in Ballsbridge. But it was the hours that clinched it. I had the evening off every single day of the week. I couldn't imagine such freedom.

There was just one problem. I hadn't the courage to tell the Everalls I was leaving. I lied, and said my mother had died, and that I was needed in Wexford. And I felt so guilty when the family showered me with sympathy.

I never told the couple I'd been in a laundry. I never told anyone – not for years. If ever I slipped up and mentioned a convent, I'd say, 'I was going to be a nun, but I changed my mind.' Anything, rather than tell the truth. If they knew I'd been a Magdalene woman I thought they'd get rid of me for sure.

I had spent my wages on clothes and shoes, so by the time I arrived in Ballsbridge I had some decent dresses. I was 17 and more confident in myself. It wasn't that I'd forgotten my experience in the laundry – I never have – but I was determined to put it all behind me and to start enjoying life.

I liked working for my new bosses, the Murrays. I cleaned the house and did all the cooking. I was good at this by then. They were an older couple, and their children had grown up. Their son got married soon after I started work there. He was so happy on his wedding day that he threw me 30 shillings as a tip. I was over the moon!

I spent a lot of time looking out of the window, dreaming and watching life go by, and I'd noticed there were other young people living on the same street as me. There was this girl with long dark hair who looked really nice. Soon we got to chatting through the window.

Her name was Marie Manee. She was at college. I said I had come to Dublin to work, but I never mentioned my background. I didn't dare, but anyway it didn't seem to matter to Marie. She liked me. I could see she was from a respectable family, but she just accepted me. She asked me to join her and her friends on a night of dancing.

'What will I wear?' I asked her, and she said, 'I bought some netting from Hickeys recently. I've made it into a stiff petticoat, and it's great under my dresses. Why don't you do the same?'

I dressed with care that first night, stuffing my bra with toilet paper. She introduced me to this whole gang, but Marie and a boy called Brian Travers became my best friends of all. We went to the Olympic Ballroom, the Four Provinces, The National and the Irish Club in Parnell Square, where that hostel had been. You name it, we danced it.

The only trouble was that I had to be in at 11 o'clock each night, so I couldn't catch the last bus home with the rest of them. That was difficult when you were in the middle of a conversation with someone.

'You have to be in at 11? That's an hour earlier than Cinderella for Christ's sake,' said Brian one day.

I didn't mind. For me the freedom was amazing. Not that I took it for granted. There was always that fear of being caught and taken back to the laundry. I was frightened that I might do something silly, or forget where I was and be found wandering the streets. Then, I might be dumped back with the nuns.

I've never been a drinker. All my life, it's been a rule with me. I don't drink so that I always know where I was the night before, and what I was doing. It's a fear of being hauled in by the Gardaí and ending up back with the nuns. And because of that I've never broken the pledge not to drink that I took at my confirmation, and I've never been in trouble with the police.

CHAPTER 43

DIANE

A FEW YEARS later I tracked down my long lost foster sister, Betty, who was living in Rathmines on the outskirts of Dublin. I went round to see her, and she joined me and my friends on some of our evenings out. One evening she mentioned that my mother had been in touch with Mrs Jordan.

'Is she in Ireland then?' I asked.

'No, no. She lives in Manchester.'

'Are you sure?'

'Oh yes. I noticed a letter from her, and I copied down the address for you. Do you want to write to her?'

I thought about it. But decided it would be better if I simply went to England and turned up on her doorstep. I was quite sure she would welcome me. Why wouldn't she when I was her long lost child? So I saved the money, gave in my notice, and brimming with a mixture of fear and excitement I took the boat and the train to England.

I was so nervous when I arrived at the house. I was shaking when I knocked on the door, but it was an old lady who answered. I asked if my mother was there, but she said, 'No dear, she's moved.'

'Oh.' I turned away, close to tears.

'But I have her address here somewhere,' said the woman, beckoning me into her hall. She rifled through the pages of a notebook, and said, 'Here we are.' And she wrote it down for me.

I walked the mile or so to the other address feeling tired and hungry, my case feeling heavier by the minute. This time, I knocked more tentatively. The woman who answered the door was young. Much younger than I'd expected. She looked lovely, and had curly hair like mine. 'Yes?' she said. 'Can I help you?'

'Hello. Are you Mam?' She put her hand to her mouth in shock. 'I mean, are you Greta?'

'Yeah. And who's asking?'

'I'm Diane. I mean Dinah.'

She looked up and down the street anxiously, then she pulled me inside saying, 'Well come in, why don't you. Hurry, before someone sees you.'

She took me through to the kitchen, and put the kettle on, making tea without asking me whether I wanted it or not. Though of course I did. We stood in silence for a while. Then handing me a mug of tea, she motioned me to sit at the table and joined me. 'I know you are after coming here to see me,' she paused. 'And that's grand. Sure it is. But when Michael . . .'

'Michael?'

'My husband. When he comes in from work, you are my niece. Is that clear?'

'But I'm your daughter!'

She put her finger to her lips. 'Shush. Don't be saying that. I'm a respectable married woman now.'

'Oh.'

'And my boys are your cousins. Is that clear?'

'Your boys?'

'I have two – *legitimate* – children now,' she said with obvious pride.

I nodded miserably. I got it. I was just the bastard daughter she'd rather didn't exist.

Whenever I had thought about my mother, which was often, I had imagined our meeting, and how happy it would be. Yet it was obvious she would rather I was anywhere else in the world but in her kitchen. And that made me terribly sad. So sad, I find it hard to put into words.

She let me stay in the house for a few days, but it was so horribly awkward. The boys were very sweet, and her husband was polite to me, but clearly confused as to why I was there. I hardly dared open my mouth, and every time I did my mother would tense up, terrified I would let slip who I was and why I was there.

Times had been hard for her when I was born, but they were much better for her now. Surely she could have welcomed me, and made up to me for abandoning me as a baby? Instead, she got me out of the house as soon as she possibly could.

She found a job for me with a Jewish family, who worked me hard. They had me scrubbing steps, and working all hours. That didn't bother me too much; I was used to hard work, but I was disappointed and annoyed with my mother because she made no effort to see me, so as soon as I had saved enough money for my fare, I left. I didn't even tell Mam I was going. I couldn't bear to see the relief on her face, so I just got the boat and found my own way home.

CHAPTER 44

DIANE

I MOVED IN to Betty's flat in Rathmines and, with her encouragement, got out of domestic service and started working in catering. I've done that ever since. Over the years I worked in some of Dublin's best hotels including The Shelbourne on St Stephen's Green.

During this time I'd met William Croghan. We met, first, at the Tayto crisp factory where I had a holiday job, but we got to know each other through the Olympic Ballroom. He asked me to dance and when it was lady's choice, I asked him! I was 17 then, and we married four years later in 1961.

By 1965 we had four children including twin girls. Life wasn't easy. We lived in a two-roomed flat in Golden Lane in Dublin and, try as we might, could not get a house from the corporation. They said, 'You haven't enough children. There are people on the list with six and seven children.'

We decided to leave the country. My husband became a lay apostle with the Christian Brothers, looking after Indians on a reservation in Burns Lake, in British Columbia, Canada. This was right in the middle of nowhere. It was a mad adventure but we enjoyed it.

After some good and some more difficult years there, my husband became lonely for Dublin, so we came home and lived with my mother-in-law for a while before we eventually got a house off the corporation. It was mad really. I went away because I didn't have enough children to get a house; I came home with the same number of children, and they hand us one. Once we had that, we decided to have more children and ended up with eight.

Six or seven years ago, I saw Mam again. She was dying and an aunt, Kathleen, who I didn't know existed, said to her, 'What about Dinah?' My half-brother, young Michael, heard this and said, 'Who is Dinah?'

Aunt Kathleen told him about me, and how I had been to Manchester when he was a small boy. He said, 'You knew about this all the time, and you never told me that I had a sister in Ireland?'

'It was your mother's wishes,' Aunt Kathleen said. 'She was desperate to keep it from you.'

Michael wanted to get in touch, so they wrote to me via Mrs Jordan, telling me that my mother wasn't well and asking me to visit. That was a terrible shock, even though I hadn't seen her for years. I got in touch with Michael, and he sent for me and paid my fare.

He met me at the airport, and we shook hands, awkwardly. Then, after examining each other, we hugged. It was strange seeing the little boy I'd met all those years ago now grown-up.

'She won't last long,' he said, as he carried my case across to the car park.

I went straight to the hospital, and there she was on the bed.

An old woman. Michael said, 'Go over and say goodbye to her.'

'She won't know me,' I said.

'Ah, but she will.'

So I went over and held her hand, and she pulled me towards her and whispered in my ear. 'I'm sorry Diane.'

'That's alright,' I said, thinking this was a bit late for apologies.

Then, looking me in the eye, she said, 'Will you find Theresa?'

'Theresa?'

She nodded. And shortly afterwards, she died. I told Michael what she'd said and he said, 'Theresa? Who the fuck is Theresa?'

'It must be another child,' said Aunt Kathleen. 'I did always wonder.'

When I got back to Ireland, I contacted the organisation Barnardo's. We found out that six years after my mother had escaped from the county home she had become pregnant again. She had Theresa in Dublin, but abandoned her in a place for illegitimate children. Theresa had been locked in an industrial school for 14 years there because she was destitute, and at 16 she had been sent to the Mercy Hospital in Cork to do domestic service.

I made contact with Theresa. She was living with her three daughters in the West of Ireland, and they all came to Dublin to stay with me. When I answered the door, we just stared at each other, trying to find a similarity between us. But we couldn't. Theresa is shorter than me, and stouter. She has short black hair, and I went grey very young.

We got on well, though we are very different. She's a private person, and she doesn't dwell on the past or tell it to other people. She's quiet compared to me. But then, I'm a mouth on hinges. I think I'm making up for all those years of silence.

*

My husband and I are now separated, but we're good friends. He lives nearby, as do most of my children and grandchildren. Two of my sons are writers. Alan wrote a book, and another son lives in Los Angeles and writes for film. I'm proud of them, but then I'm proud of them all.

I'm pleased that they turned out well, because when they were small I found it hard to show them love. I was never shown it as a child and I didn't know how. I couldn't even hug them.

When all the news came out about the Magdalene laundry, I decided to tell them I had been in one. I thought they'd think less of me, but they just took it. Then one of my daughters heard from her friend, the politician Mary Lou McDonald, that there was a group called Magdalene Survivors Together. I rang the number, spoke to Steven O'Riordan, and went along to a meeting in a hotel in Dublin. And bless him, Steven did a fantastic job for us. For a young man to give up his time like that is quite something, and he did give us so much time.

It has been good meeting all the other women in the group. We have different experiences, and a different way of looking at what happened, but we've become close. I think of them all as good friends.

I was in the Dáil when Enda Kenny apologised. It was such a great day, even though Summerhill was not included in the apology. I trusted Steven. I knew he would go on fighting for me and he did. He applied to the Department of Justice, and by the time we met Justice Quirke it was decided that people who had been at Summerhill were eligible for the scheme of compensation. This was all thanks to Steven. I divided all the money I was awarded between my children, so it's all grand.

I'm not bitter. I'm still a Catholic and I go to Mass, but only because I enjoy singing in the choir. I don't blame the Church for what happened to me. It was the fault of the individual nuns, yet maybe they were victims too. Many mothers wanted a son to become a priest and a daughter a nun. It made them look good, and society treated them with respect. I think parents forced their children into it, and that made the nuns bitter and cruel.

I blame my mother too, to a point. I know times were hard, but I can't let her off the hook. I've had my own share of bad times but we worked for our money. I worked to keep my children in food. There were times we hadn't anything, and needed charity. But I would never abandon my children. Not in a million years.

CHAPTER 45

MARIE

ALL MY LIFE I have been called a tramp. I've been called a whore, and I've been told I was dirty. And I said that to Justice Quirke, when he heard our stories that day in the Commissions Office. I will never forget it. Because I had never told my story, and I didn't know if I could.

We were sitting round a big table, and Justice Quirke said, 'I know you're all nervous. I know this is hard. So just take your time. And if you have to stop to collect yourselves, that's fine too. There's no hurry.'

There was a new woman in my group called Nancy. She'd sat down beside Justice Quirke, but she didn't want to tell her story first. She was nervous. But in the end she did, and it was so sad that we all had to brush away tears.

Nancy was in an orphanage before she was in a laundry. She lost her teeth. She saw a girl accidentally kill herself trying to escape. Oh my God! It was just terrible, what Nancy went through. She was so good the way she came out with it.

Everybody cried, including Steven, and there was even a tear in Justice Quirke's eye. There was a break after Nancy's story. There had to be because everyone was so upset. I was sitting there thinking, *I've never been in a group telling my story before. How can I do it?*

When it came to me, I was shaking with nerves. I didn't know where to start, but then I just did.

I was lashed into the Good Shepherd laundry in Sundays Well in Cork, in 1972, when I was 12 years old. It was a Sunday evening, and I was squashed into our little Mini Minor with my brothers and sisters. I thought my mam and dad were taking us for a spin. We turned up through this big gate and drove up a lane with trees either side. We came to this huge red brick building which had three parts to it. I'd never seen anything like it.

My father parked the car, then telling my brothers and sisters to stay put, he and my mother took me up these big steps to the front door. We rang the bell and a nun opened the door. She led us through this archway with stained glass either side, and she showed us into a tiny office like a little cell with a desk and chairs. There was another nun sitting there, behind the desk. She asked my parents to sit down on the two chairs. I just stood there, squirming. The nun looked me slowly up and down, and said, 'So *this* is Marie.'

I don't remember the conversation. But my parents couldn't get out of the place quickly enough. They didn't hug me goodbye. Just waved, turned and almost ran. I do remember that. I was too scared to ask why I was there, how long I was staying or what I was there to do.

'You're 12, Marie. Is that right?'

'Yes.'

'Yes *Mother*,' said the nun, and I thought, *but you don't look like a mother to me.* Not in that horrible nun's habit. 'I'm Mother Patricia,' she said. 'Can you read and write child?'

I blushed. Because the truth was, I couldn't. I'd never done well at my lessons. The teacher had called me a dunce, and I really had no interest in school. I felt the nuns who taught me were very hard on me.

'Well Marie, you won't need to read and write here. We'll put you in with the other penitents.'

No more school suited me just fine, but what were penitents, I wondered. Mother Patricia showed me up to a room with three beds in it. 'We have a routine here, and you have to keep to it. Do you understand?'

I nodded.

'I said, do *you* understand.'

'Yes. Yes Mother,' I said.

Later, I met the two women I was to share with. They were both terribly old, and seemed very holy. They were forever kneeling beside their beds and saying their prayers. They didn't take any notice of me.

It felt so strange, that night, getting into a bed by myself, when normally I shared with my sister. I was so worried about what would happen to me that I barely slept a wink. It didn't help that one of the old women snored.

I could barely open my eyes when we were woken the next day, early, for chapel. Then we went to the refectory for breakfast. The food was okay – some gooey porridge, then bread. I was extremely hungry, so I just ate. A nun sat at the top end of the room, on a throne thing. One of the girls read a story from the Bible, but she mumbled and I couldn't hear it against the scrape of spoons and the sound of someone coughing.

After breakfast we were put to cleaning, which was hard.

Then it was down to the laundry. I remember the smell. I didn't know what it was, that first day, but I was to learn it was the stink of starch. It would catch at the back of your throat and stay with you all day. And at night-times too. It was a musty smell, like rotten flour. The sheets would be soaked in it, then we put them onto this big roller. There were two girls behind it, and me and another girl in front. I was told to fold everything nicely and make sure the creases on the sheets were in the right place. Then we had to put the sheets through again and again until they were dry.

We took turns to wash the priests' clothes, and the nuns' clothes too. We would soak them in a huge bucket. We'd poke them around with a big stick, then wash them all down. And this went on all day. Nobody explained how long I would stay there, or even why I was there, and I didn't ask. I thought somebody would tell me soon enough.

Mother Assumpta was in charge of the laundry. She'd sit there, watching us through her thick glasses. You couldn't slow down in your work, and if she saw you speak to someone she would shout, her face going dark red. I was terrified of her.

The nuns were always reminding me that I was a penitent. They kept telling me I had to atone for my sins. I put up with this for a while, then, finally, asked Mother Patricia what I had done wrong.

'You know exactly what you did,' she said. 'You were a temptation to your grandfather, and you made up stories against him.'

That was so unfair, it made me cry. I *never* made up stories. I told the truth, but nobody believed me. *That's* the truth.

CHAPTER 46

MARIE

I WAS BORN in Castlelyons, in East County Cork, in 1960. I had two brothers and later, three younger sisters, and my parents hated me. The only person who loved me was my grandfather on my father's side

'You're my little girl, Marie,' he would say. 'My little pet.' And I stayed his little girl, even after my three sisters were born. 'It's still you that I love the best,' he'd say. He'd say that in front of Catherine, my next sister down. And when I was on Granda's knee, she would tug at his trousers and ask him to pick her up too. But he'd just pat her on the head, and tell her to go off and play.

Sometimes Mammy walked me the mile and a half to his house and left me there for the day. I loved it. I'd play with his two collie dogs, and try and teach them tricks. Granda would hold my hand as we walked across the fields. I loved that. I loved the attention, because I wasn't getting any of it at home. But when I was five years old it all went wrong.

Granda asked could he could keep me all weekend, and Mammy agreed.

'Anything to get rid of her,' she said.

I was pleased. Granda had a small farm, and he'd told me there were two new calves.

He took me up to show them to me. After I'd petted them for a while, I ran off into the hay barn, and made a house for myself out of the bales. I played outside all day and in the evening, after tea, Granda took me onto his knee as usual.

Then he said, 'Time for bed, Marie, and he carried me upstairs, undressed me and got into bed beside me. He put his arms round me and held me close. 'You're my little pet,' he said. And snuggling there, I felt safe.

But I wasn't safe. Granda said he loved me. He said, 'Do you love me too, little Marie.' And of course I did. But I didn't know what love meant. Granda said it meant me holding his penis. He said it meant him putting his penis between my legs. And when he grunted, and went red and all scary, he said, 'You're a good girl.' Then he told me to stop crying.

I didn't want to spend the night there anymore, but Mammy made me. Every weekend she would drag me there, and every night he would take me to his bed. I liked him hugging me because nobody else ever did. But when he started to fumble between my legs, I would tense up and say, 'No. No Granda, you're hurting me.' But he did it anyway.

I hated school, but I hated weekends more.

My First Holy Communion day should have been happy. It should have been the best day of my life. That's what the nuns told us at school. We would be accepted into the Church by Jesus. I was so excited. But one day, when I'd walked home from school, Granda was there. He handed me this beautiful white dress, with a high waist flowing into a full lacy skirt.

'I bought this for you Marie,' he said. 'For your Holy Communion.'

Catherine stroked the dress, and said, 'It's not fair! I want one too.'

She was always jealous of me. She thought I had a great time with Granda, and a good life altogether.

'Try it on,' said Granda. I did. And everyone said I looked beautiful, like an angel. All innocent and pure. And all I could think was, *I'm no angel. I'm dirty.* And Granda knew that. I didn't know what to think. He just stood there, smiling. Then he winked at me, as if I was happy that we shared this secret.

The day came. The other girls looked lovely. They said I did too. 'Where did you get such a beautiful dress?' they asked. It was nicer than theirs. I watched them swirl around, and wished I could feel happy like them. But I couldn't. I don't think Jesus did welcome me that day. We'd had our first confession, and I hadn't told the priest what I'd done with my grandfather. I didn't know how to, because I didn't know what it was.

That's the reason I didn't tell anyone what was happening. At least not during the first years. I hoped they would guess. I begged and begged Mammy not to send me to Granda anymore. 'I hate staying over,' I said. But she didn't ask me why.

'You should be pleased he wants you there,' she said. 'He's the only one who does.'

That hurt me, but it was true. I don't know why Mammy hated me. I suppose it's because I was always in trouble as a child. I was always running away up the fields and hiding there. I wouldn't come back for hours and hours, and when I did come home I'd get hammered.

'I'll put a stop to that behaviour if it kills me,' said Mammy, hitting me with an old black belt that had once been on a machine. She left welts on my legs, and on my arms and my back.

None of us had it easy. We all had to walk three miles to school in the rain and the wind, and we were all sent there with no sandwiches for our dinner. We all felt that leather strap, and there was little love in the home. But I was the one they came down on the hardest.

Mammy was no angel. I wonder, now, if something happened to her when she was a child. I never met her parents. Never, and she wouldn't talk about them. I'd ask her about her childhood sometimes, but she said, 'Shut your fucking mouth. Mind your business.'

She would have sex with other men, and she didn't care if we knew it. Paddy, a neighbour from down the road, would come up and she had sex with the milkman too. We would hear them upstairs. We'd hear her laughing and saying, 'Stop it!'

Daddy never stood up to her, and he didn't stick up for me either. He had a good job with the Electricity Supply Board, but at home he was quiet, unless he had taken drink. You'd avoid him then.

I did tell about my granda in the end. Mammy was telling me to go to him for the weekend. And I was begging and begging her not to send me. And I told her why. But it did no good.

'Just shut your dirty mouth,' she said, slapping me hard across the face, leaving an imprint of her fingers. 'You disgust me. You're bold. You're making up stories out of spite.'

I go through that in my head, all the time. Why would I make up something so horrible? Why would she not believe me?

Granda died when I was 11 years old. I was glad. I hated him, and now he couldn't hurt me anymore. But the odd thing was, I missed him too.

CHAPTER 47

MARIE

I KNOW I was wild when I was 12. I'd left national school and been put in the Loreto Convent Secondary School. I lasted two weeks. Then I was sent to the local technical college but that didn't work out either and a social worker was called in. She was the one who said maybe I should go to a laundry.

Home was no heaven, but it was an awful lot better than the laundry. It was just so lonely and sad there. You looked out of the window and you could see the whole city of Cork down below you and up towards Sundays Well. You could see it, but you were locked away.

There were a lot of girls my age and a bit older there, but they tried to keep us away from each other. You were put in a circle of 12 which was led by an older woman called an auxiliary. We ate on the same table as the others who were in our circle, and sat with them in the evening for recreation. All of them were a lot older than me. That made it all lonelier than ever.

It didn't do to get ill in the laundry. If you weren't well, you went to the infirmary at 10 a.m. and they gave you some medicine, and sent you back to the laundry. You had to be dying before they would send for a doctor.

I was there one day for a cough. There was a girl in the queue with a terrible tummy ache, she was bent double. She asked to see a doctor, but Sister Bernadette said, 'We can't call him just for you.' Then they sent her back to work.

I didn't see her for a while, but later I heard that she'd had her appendix out. She was in hospital for 10 days. Someone said she nearly died.

I had been in the laundry for around nine months, when we were sitting doing our work after tea, making rosary beads for the nuns to sell. I was accused of being too slow. I was tired and fed up, and I started to cry.

This girl, Breda, noticed. She was in another circle, but she came up to me as we made our way to the stairs to queue for bed. 'Are you okay?' she whispered.

'I can't stand this place a minute longer.'

'Nor me. Let's escape!' she said with a glint in her eye.

I laughed when she said that, and agreed at once. We didn't spend long planning our escape, and really it wasn't so hard. The doors were locked, but there was always a window we could get through. Once we were in the front of the building there was nothing to stop us walking down the lane and out of the gate. But we weren't in luck. Someone noticed we were missing, and we'd only just reached the road when we were hauled back in by the Gardaí.

I knew we were for it, and we were. It was out with the scissors and off with our hair. Mother Patricia hacked at it, leaving it in ugly tufts. It was terrible. It gave me nightmares, and I have never let anyone cut my hair since. I just let it grow. I have never, in my life, been to a hairdresser. I just couldn't.

Every month, on a Sunday afternoon, the Mini Minor would come up the lane with Daddy, a brother and two of my sisters on board. Mammy never came. Daddy always said, 'She can't Marie. Someone has to stay at home and take care of little Patricia.'

We didn't talk much. It was as if I'd forgotten how. I remember walking around the grounds, and taking them to the grave of Little Nellie of Holy God; a girl who had died at four years old in 1908. She'd been in St Finbarr's Industrial School – the building on the other side of the convent from the laundry. The nuns were always talking about her, telling us how blessed we were that her remains were in the convent graveyard. 'She had the mystical gift of discernment,' they said.

That meant she understood what communion meant, and she had visions that she played with the baby Jesus. Bishops went to see her, and the Pope knew her story. She was always sick and in pain, and she died of tuberculosis.

Catherine loved that story. By this time she was 12, and had just gone into first year in the Loreto Convent School. She was worried that she didn't have a bra yet. 'The other girls do,' she said. 'They laugh at me.' I went to the dormitory and fetched one of my old ones for her. Her face lit up. She has said since that it was like winning the Lotto.

We never had a real conversation. Nobody spoke about why I was there or when I could come home again. And though it was nice to know I had not been forgotten, when the Mini Minor went down that drive again, with Catherine and Martina waving through the windows, I would stand on the steps with Mother Patricia feeling more lonely that ever.

The laundry was hard for me, but it was even worse for girls who had nobody to visit them, like the girls who had come from the industrial schools. The nuns felt they owned them, and could do what they liked to them. They would be blamed for everything. If we were caught talking, for example, they were the ones who would be pounced on and punished. I could see that wasn't fair.

After two years of hard work, with only Sundays off, I felt I just had to get out of there. I thought I'd go mad if I stayed a day longer. So, together with another girl, Mona, I planned my escape. And this time we got away. We hitched all the way to Dublin, and we ended up in a hostel. Then she moved somewhere else and I didn't see her again.

I don't know what happened to her, but I ran out of luck. Daddy tracked me down. The nuns in the laundry had contacted him to tell him of my escape so he came looking for me. I have never seen him so cross.

'What do you think you were doing?' he said, pulling me roughly by the arm. 'Do you know what can happen to young girls wandering around Dublin on their own? Do you want to get yourself killed?'

'I'm fine, so I am,' I said, pulling away from him. But in truth I'd no idea how I was going to survive.

'You're coming with me,' he said, 'And we're off back to the nuns.'

And with that, he half dragged me to Sean McDermott Street in Dublin, and to a Magdalene laundry run by the Religious Sisters of Our Lady of Charity. My freedom had been short-lived.

CHAPTER 48

MARIE

AT FIRST, THE convent in Sean McDermott Street seemed exactly the same as the convent in Sundays Well. You went through a huge door of a red brick building, through an archway and into a tiny office. Then I was led out through the back of the building to a yard. There was a big high wall, and the laundry was one side and there was a smaller building on the other side. They took me there, and said, 'This is where you will be living Marie.'

Downstairs there was a big table where we ate all our meals. And upstairs were these great big dormitories. It was the usual rigmarole. 'There's a routine here, you have to follow it.' 'You're here to atone for your sins.' And, 'You can't talk in the refectory or the laundry.' I didn't need telling. I could recite all that off by heart.

But soon I realised this laundry was a holiday camp compared to the last one. For one thing, everyone in our building was young. There was nobody older than 16. For another, we didn't have to work all day. We didn't have to make rosary beads or scapulas, and we had more free time. Sometimes we played our version of tennis in the yard.

Justice Quirke started writing something down when I said that. And Elizabeth, a woman in our group, said, 'That would be because of Vatican II. I think the nuns were told they should treat us as individuals, and not as if we were nuns in the making.' She said she was in a laundry at that time, and things began to get better for her as well. 'We had guitar lessons,' she said, 'and, occasionally, they showed films.'

'I remember that,' I said. 'If there was any kissing they put a sheet over the screen.' Everyone laughed at that, even Justice Quirke.

But the work was still as terrible. The nun in charge in the laundry, Sister Anne, didn't let us get away with anything. She was small and fat with a round red face. She'd sit on that throne with her crucifix swinging from her waist, looking like a blown up snowman. Nothing got past Sister Anne.

The food was the same as in the Good Shepherd: mince and bacon and cabbage, never anything fancy, and at tea maybe a boiled egg and a slice of bread.

'That's better than we had,' said Nancy, and the other older women in the group agreed with her.

But the really great thing about Sean McDermott Street was that we could get out every now and then, and go to the shop on the corner. We had pocket money for sweets. I loved fizzy bears.

We got away with more too. The girls who worked in the packing room sometimes found a cigarette left in a jacket. And one brave girl cadged the odd one from a man we'd see on the street. We'd wait until it was dark, then we'd walk down to the end of the yard, climb over some steps in the wall, to a bit of grass between the wall and the next building. We were hidden there. That's where we'd have our sneaky smoke.

I found it hard to get on with the other girls. There were two who seemed nice. They asked me if I'd like to go for a smoke with them. I said I would, but when we'd gone over the wall, they jumped on me and pulled my knickers down. They said I was a whore and they were rough with me. I found it hard to trust any of the girls after that. And all I wanted was a friend.

In the summer they would take us away to Skerries in North Dublin for the weekend. We stayed in a big country house which was let out to groups of teenagers. The scouts sometimes went there, I heard. We had a good time, simply being free. We walked round the fields just talking. I loved looking at the trees as it got dark. I imagined they had heads. It was fun, with the whole gang of us there.

One Saturday morning, when I was 15, I took it into my head to leave the laundry. I noticed that the door was open, and took the opportunity. I had no possessions, no money, and not a clue where to go. I hung around the streets all day, and in the evening a man came and started chatting to me. He asked me to go drinking with him. He seemed okay, so I did, but I wasn't used to the drink and I ended up falling around the place, drunk and senseless.

He slapped me, and tried to force me into having sex. He called me a whore and a slut, and I was crying when he finished. He just left me there, slumped in an alleyway. I'm crying at the memory. I'm so ashamed, telling that.

'I don't know what it is about me,' I said to Justice Quirke. 'Why do these things happen to me?'

*

After a few days I thumbed a lift home to my village. I can't say Mammy and Daddy were pleased to see me, but they let me stay. I just hung around there while they tried to decide what to do with me.

After a few weeks, I began to feel sick. This went on. I didn't know what was wrong with me, and after a week or two my mammy took me to the doctor. He prodded me and poked me, then called my mother in.

'She's pregnant,' he said.

My mother's face was thunder. And the minute we got home she beat me. 'You're sex mad so you are,' she said. 'I always knew it! And you blaming your poor grandfather . . .'

After that, there was no way she was letting me stay at home. 'You've brought shame to this family,' she said. And before I knew it, my bag was packed and it was into Bessborough convent with me.

CHAPTER 49

MARIE

BESSBOROUGH WAS ANOTHER laundry, and it was run by yet another order of nuns – the Sacred Heart Sisters. There was a mother and baby's home there as well, and that's where I was put. It was so hard, knowing the baby was growing in my belly and being reminded of the violence that got it there. All the time I was pregnant I worked with the babies. It was a lot better than working in the laundry. But then, anything was better than that.

We worked in twos, doing day shifts, then night shifts, and we had maybe 10 babies to look after. Doing days, we'd be up at 7 a.m. to get our breakfast, then we'd rush into the babies in time to give them their eight o'clock bottles. When we'd fed them, it was time to scrub the nursery and the corridors and then it was 12 noon, and time for our dinner. We rushed that and got back for the next feed, and so it went on all day. We had no time to think. For all that, I found the nights the worst. By four in the morning I'd be dead on my feet.

But I loved the babies. There was one that I got really close to. Her mum had gone, and I looked after her for nine months. Pauline was her name. I nearly raised that baby. I watched her learn to sit up, to crawl and then to walk. I'll never forget those first three steps she took. I was so proud of her.

We had such a bond, the two of us. Every time I went on duty, she'd see me and she'd smile and hold her arms out to be picked up. I felt like she was mine. It nearly broke my heart when she left. But by that time, I had a baby of my own.

My pains started in my back. I didn't know what they were, but the nun in charge examined me and said the pain was contractions. She sent me into the labour ward, or the room they called the labour ward. It had a hard couch in it, like the examnation table you see in doctor's surgeries, and an ordinary plain cot, and not much else. The nun in charge there was called Sister Martha, and I will never, ever forget her, the bitch.

The pains were tearing me apart, and I started roaring. And Sister Martha roared at me.

'Shut your mouth!' she said. 'Do you not realise there are other patients here apart from you? Do you want to disturb everyone?'

I will never forget the pain. It was unbearable and nobody cared. There was no such thing as pain relief at Bessborough. Epidural? Are you joking me? There was no gas and no mask. There wasn't even an aspirin. Yet this was 1976 – not the dark ages. And I was lying there, in agony, for 24 endless hours. The worst time was when Sister went for her tea and left me alone. I was terrified for my life. When she came back, I said, 'Please Sister, help me!'

'Ah Marie,' she said, looking at me as if I was dirt. 'You should have thought of the consequences before getting yourself in this mess. Tell me, was the two minutes of pleasure worth all this?'

And I thought, *Pleasure? Does she think I liked being raped? Does she know anything?* After a while she had a look, down there, to see how I was doing, swore under her breath and went out again. A while later, she brought in some men with a stretcher. They put me in an ambulance and took me to St Finbarr's Hospital. Nobody told me why. I was so scared, I thought I was going to die.

When we arrived at the hospital, they pushed the stretcher into a room full of metal equipment and I realised that this was a real labour ward. The nurses were kind, they held my hand and whispered encouragement, but I worried when they called a doctor and said I needed forceps. Was something wrong? When the doctor pulled my baby into the world, I tried to sit up.

'What is it? What have I had?' I lifted my arms, waiting for them to hand me my baby. But they didn't.

'It's a boy,' they said, then they took him away.

'Please, can I see him?'

'I'm sorry Marie. We're just keeping an eye on him.'

I lay there, exhausted and bewildered, and I cried for my baby. Was he dying? Or were they keeping him away because I was 15 and unmarried and an unfit mother? I spent a few days in hospital, during which I had my sixteenth birthday. Not that anyone cared. Then I was carted back to Bessborough, and put in the hospital section of the convent.

There was a ward of six beds there. The nun in charge was called Sister Anthony. I will never forget her because she was kind to me. She supplied me with all the pads I needed, and she made sure I had pain killers when I needed them. She gave me sweets too. Of all the nuns I met, she was the one person who seemed to take to me. She was better than any mother, and certainly better than mine.

She brought my baby to me. I called him Paul Anthony. He had black curly hair, and he was so tiny. I tried to hold him, but I was afraid I would drop him. I knew I should love him, but I was tired and sore and for those first days I felt numb. I didn't breastfeed. Nobody suggested that I should.

The Sisters said I should give Paul Anthony up for adoption. It was what my parents wanted, and they said it was for the best. The way I saw it, I had no choice. So I signed the papers.

When I started to feel better, I wanted Paul Anthony with me so I could know him before he was adopted. He was kept in the nursery and I'd go in there to see him, but the nurses would send me away.

'He's asleep,' they'd say. 'And you mustn't disturb the babies.'

I tried and tried to sneak in, but they always caught me. I didn't get to know him, and that was hard. And when he was just three weeks old they said he was ready to go.

I will never forget saying goodbye to Paul Anthony. It was lunchtime. Sister gave me a little blue suit, and said, 'Will you dress him in this, please Marie.'

I cried as I put his little arms and legs into the suit and he looked up at me with those big eyes. I tried to hide my tears, but it was hard. He was mine, and it hit me that I would never see him again.

I didn't know where he was going. Sister had told me they had found him a good home, and that he would have a great life, but they always said that. When he was dressed they made me carry him up the corridor, then hand him to a nun. He started screaming. Words cannot describe how I felt, letting go of him that last time.

*

When I got to that part of my story, I could not go on. I threw myself forwards onto the table and starting sobbing. My heart was breaking all over again. I thought of my story, of Nancy's story, and all the other stories. It was too much to take.

Justice Quirke said, 'It's alright Marie. Take your time.'

'I can't do it,' I said. 'I just can't.'

'Ah go on,' said Elizabeth, putting an arm round me. 'We want to hear.'

Steven agreed. 'You'll be okay. It's your one chance, and it's for the compensation. Better to get it over.'

Someone handed me a tissue. I wiped my eyes, and took a deep breath.

'This is so hard,' I said, sniffing. 'Losing a baby, well, it's the worst thing ever.'

There were murmurs of agreement.

'Are you alright now?' asked Justice Quirke.

I nodded.

When I'd handed Paul Anthony over I rushed to the window to see if I could catch a last glimpse of him. I watched for ages, but I didn't see anything. I don't know whether he went with a priest, a nun, a social worker or his new parents.

Not a day goes by when I don't think about Paul Anthony. I wonder, what does he look like now? Now that he is a grown man of 38. I'll never know. I wonder did he go to America, like lots of babies did in the Seventies. I heard that nearly 100 went from Bessborough over the years. I wonder, is he happy. I've never tried to trace him. As I see it, I don't have the right. I signed the adoption papers to hand him over. It wouldn't be fair to try and find him now.

I carried him for nine months, I gave birth to him, I knew him for three weeks, I dressed him when he went away, but

I have no claims on him. If he wanted to know about me, he would have found me. That's the way I look at it. It's up to him. But the pain never goes away. You'll always be looking around you, thinking, is that my son, there?

CHAPTER 50

MARIE

SOON AFTER PAUL Anthony was adopted, the nuns let me leave Bessborough. I went home for a while, but I wasn't wanted there. My mother wanted me out, and the truth was I could never settle at home. A social worker visited, and they agreed it would be better if I went to a rehabilitation centre in the North Mall in Cork. It was a hostel for girls.

Life soon took on a routine. Each morning, a bus would take a group of us to work. I went to a factory in Douglas where they made stockings. I was in charge of sorting the stockings into pairs.

We started work at nine in the morning, and finished at five. It wasn't a laundry, but it was nearly as bad. The pay was paltry. When we finished work, it was back to the hostel, where the woman made us our dinner. Then we went upstairs to our beds. I shared a room with three other girls, and though we got along alright they didn't really become friends.

I left that place when I was almost 17. I just took off, and ended up sleeping rough. It was a bad time and I hit the bottle.

Things spiralled out of control. I started hitching lifts, and I met a truck driver from Galway. He was a lot older than me; probably in his fifties, but I liked that. I felt he could look after me, and he did, for a while.

I would go up to the north with him, or to Galway or Kerry or Tralee, and we'd sleep in the bunk. We'd be together for six days, then he would go home for a day or two. He was married. I didn't care so long as he was good to me. And he was.

It wasn't a relationship. I don't know, really, what you would call it, but I stayed with him for quite a while. Then we broke up. I don't remember why. His wife never knew about me.

I fell pregnant again when I was 17. This was 1979, when contraceptives were still illegal in Ireland. The father came from County Cork, and he was another truck driver. That wasn't just a coincidence. I went for them because I liked roaming around the country. I was always thumbing a lift to Dublin or to Cork or Donegal. You were dry and safe on the inside of a truck. He was about fifty as well. I always felt safer with older men. I still do, I don't know why.

I kept well away from my parents, and they didn't know that I was pregnant again, and I wanted to keep it that way for as long as I could. I took myself back to Bessborough, because I didn't know where else to go. I had another boy, Johnny, or officially, John Finbar. He was gorgeous with his big blue eyes. I loved him from the moment he was born, and decided there was no way I was going to let him go.

I stayed on in Bessborough convent for six months after he was born. I saw his first smile, I heard his first babbles of speech and I watched when he learned to roll over. And all that time the nuns were trying to force me to sign the adoption papers. 'Come on Marie,' they said. 'What can you give Johnny? You've no money, no job – you've nothing, and you won't amount to anything. You haven't even the support of your family.'

That was true. I knew it, but I didn't care. I was Johnny's mother, I loved him and I would see him right. I fought to the battle for him. But the nuns didn't give up easily. Even lovely Sister Anthony told me adoption might be for the best. 'We could find him wonderful parents,' she said. 'Maybe even a doctor or a lawyer. He'll have things you could only dream about.'

Another of the Sisters suggested that I stay on at the convent to work. That made me laugh. I couldn't bear to stay a day longer than the six months. By now my parents knew about Johnny, and I wanted them to collect the two of us, but they said they wouldn't. They thought it would be sensible if I stayed on.

'Think of it, Marie,' they said. 'You'd have security there.' What they meant was, I couldn't disgrace them by getting pregnant again if I was locked safely behind those walls. It would have suited them if I'd stayed in that place for life.

One day, I noticed a taxi delivering a pregnant girl. I ran out and rapped on the car window. The driver opened it and said, 'Can I take you somewhere?'

'Well you can do me a big favour.'

'What would that be love?'

I explained that I needed to get out of the place. 'Could you please pretend to be my uncle?'

At first he wouldn't agree, but in the end I persuaded him. I told him what to say, and he went into the office and told the nuns he had come to collect me and Johnny, to take us home. They agreed, even though I didn't know him from Adam. I'll never forget being driven through those gates with my beautiful baby boy. It was like a great big weight lifted.

I ended up living with my real uncle in Glanmire, because my mother didn't want me in the house. We had our own room there, Johnny and me, but it didn't turn out well. My uncle was kind when he was sober, but when he came back from the pub it was a whole different story. He would try and push his way into my room. I'd shove the furniture against the door to stop him, but once or twice he got through and I was for it.

'You're nothing but a whore, anyway,' he'd say, those few times, as he zipped up his trousers. 'You're a disgrace to the family.'

I threatened to tell my mother.

'You do that, and it's back to the streets with you,' he said.

The social worker came out to the cottage to see me. I told her I didn't want to stay with my uncle, but she said it was my best bet. I ended up staying there for a good few months, but I lived constantly on my nerves.

Then life got better. A friend from the village, Mary, found a flat to rent in Cork. She had a baby, too, and she asked if Johnny and I would live with her there. It was perfect! I visited my parents, sometimes, and it seemed that my problems were over. But when Johnny was 18 months old I fell pregnant again. I'd been in a relationship, but when the father heard I was pregnant I didn't see him for dust.

Everything got too much. I took to the drink again and I went off, leaving Johnny with my mother. She put him into St Finbarr's Industrial School in Cork – next to the Good Shepherd's laundry. When I came home and found him missing I nearly lost my mind. It seemed so final. I had no idea how I was going to get him back.

I don't remember much about that time – I think I've blanked it out – but I do know that I wasn't thinking straight. I started hitching round the country again. I was on my way to Dublin when my pains started; I'd thumbed a lift with a man in a white van. When I realised I was in labour, I asked him to take me to a home for unmarried mothers. There was one called St Patrick's on the Navan Road.

He dumped me at this building, but it turned out to be a nursing home for old people. A nurse there called a taxi, but by the time I arrived at St Patrick's I was in the final stages of labour and ready to push. I was taken straight to the labour ward.

'Push Marie,' said the nun on duty. I was pushing and pushing but she kept on shouting, telling me to push harder still, and harder. I did. I tried so hard. But no baby was coming. After a while the nuns called an ambulance and I was taken to St James's Hospital in Dublin. They broke my waters there, to make the baby come, but nothing happened. I was shaking and shivering, and crying out with the pain.

'We'll have to give you a caesarean section,' said the nurse. 'And I think we should contact your family too.'

'No, don't,' I said, tugging at her arm. 'Please don't.'

'But you need support, Marie.'

'Please,' I said. 'I mean it. I don't want anybody to know that I'm in here.' I didn't want to tell them why, but I was terrified that if my mother found out where I was she would take this baby away from me too. And I couldn't stand that. Not after Johnny.

CHAPTER 51

MARIE

THEY PUT ME to sleep to have my caesarean section, and when I woke up I had a horrible sore tummy.

'Where am I?' I felt all woozy.

'You're in intensive care.'

'Where's my baby?' I said, as I tried to sit up.

'Careful,' said a nurse. 'You've had an incision. You'll have to move cautiously for a day or two.'

I lay down again. 'I want to see my baby.'

'You can see your baby boy soon enough,' said the nurse.

'My baby boy? I've had a boy? I want to see him now,' I said. 'I want to see my James.'

The next day the nurse came in and took my hand. 'I'm really sorry, Marie, but I'm afraid your little baby has died.'

'He's died? My baby? My James?' I just couldn't take it in. 'No! No, he can't have!' How could my baby be dead? He'd only just been born. I sobbed and sobbed, and thought I would never stop.

'Would you like to see him?' asked the nurse, and I thought,

Why couldn't I see him when he was alive? But after thinking about it for a while, I decided I did.

'Are you sure?'

I nodded. She wheeled me down to the mortuary, and the cold and damp hit me at once. He was just lying there. He looked perfect. He had these long eyelashes. He was dressed in a little robe with a rose on the front of it. I counted his tiny little fingers and wept for the life he might have had.

It was hard leaving him in that horrible room with the concrete floor. His little cradle and been pushed into a corner, as if he didn't matter, but he did. He mattered to me. I can still picture him to this day.

I don't know why my James died. Nobody ever told me. I don't know where he was buried either, or even if he was buried. I didn't think to ask. The thought of it haunts me.

It was so terrible losing James, especially after I had given away Paul Anthony. I decided, there and then, that I would get Johnny back again whatever happened. As soon as I was let out of the hospital, I went to see my mother and I pleaded and pleaded with her. I cried and screamed. I said, 'I'll do anything you want, if you'll just get him back.'

I got up early every morning, and scrubbed the floors. I made myself useful, trying to be a really good girl. I went on and on about getting Johnny back, and my mother kept saying he was fine where he was. 'You're not a fit mother,' she said. And my father said I was nothing but a whore.

In the end I wore my mother down. She signed a letter giving permission to let me take Johnny out. I went up to the convent, so full of hope, but they said my mother had to be there with me.

I begged her to come, and to my great surprise she agreed.

So the two of us hitched up to the convent and got him out. I bought some little brown rompers for him to wear. I couldn't believe how much he had changed. He had started to talk, but the sad thing was that he hadn't a clue who I was. Not at first. It took time before he was comfortable with me.

My sisters loved Johnny, especially Catherine.

'You're so lucky, Marie, to have him,' she said, jigging him up and down on her knee.

She said this so often that I asked her why she didn't just go off and get pregnant. But I knew she had been warned, time and again, not to go down the same road as me. Whenever my mother was angry with Catherine, Martina or Patricia, it was always, 'You don't want to ruin your life like your sister. You're not to go the way Marie went.'

I was always searching for love, but I looked in all the wrong places. Soon after I got Johnny back I met another truck driver. He was a lot older than me, no surprise there, but I thought he was my perfect man. I took Johnny on my travels now, and Tom was great with him. I told him how bad things were at home, and he asked me if I'd like to go to the North of Ireland and live with him.

'Aren't you married?' I asked, because he'd told me he had two daughters.

'I'm separated. The marriage broke a while back.' One of his daughters, it turned out, was the same age as me, and the other was two years younger. We got on really well, and he was wonderful with Johnny. So I went to Belfast with him. My luck seemed to be changing.

Life was good. Tom cared for Johnny as if he was his own. And when I discovered that I was pregnant again, our family felt complete. When Thomas was born, Tom was over the moon. He doted on him straight away.

'I've always wanted a son,' he said, and my heart sank a little. I thought, *But you already have one in Johnny, or as good as. You said you'd love him like your own.*

That's when things changed. Johnny got pushed aside. He was only four, and he didn't understand what he had done wrong.

I was so happy when Tom and I got married. At first, I was. I had everything I had always wanted. My own home, a man to love, and having Thomas *with* someone, with his father. That made me so proud. I felt so happy when I brought him home. And then Matthew was born and that was lovely too.

But marriage turned Tom. He liked to control me. He wouldn't even let me go to bingo. I felt imprisoned, and for me, after the laundry, there is nothing worse. But the worst of it all was that he was so hard on Johnny.

I love my sons. I love all of them, and I have never stopped loving them. But I have never been able to show it. I couldn't tell them, I can't give. I just can't. I freeze and get all shaky. I don't know why. I wanted to give them a hug, but I'd end up giving out to them.

Being unable to read and write, I couldn't tell them bedtime stories, and I couldn't help with their homework. I felt I was a bad mother.

I found it difficult living in Belfast because Tom was a protestant. When we first met that didn't seem to matter. But some of his family started to taunt me. With drink taken they called me a Fenian bastard.

'We'll throw you on the bonfire, so we will,' they said.

The marriage wasn't to last. It deteriorated and my drinking got bad again. Drink blanks everything out. Twelve years ago,

I'd had enough. The boys had almost grown up – they were aged 24, 20 and 18 – and I couldn't take any more. I left Tom. I waited for him to go off to work, then I packed my bags and was gone. I took a train to Fermoy, and stayed in a hostel for a while. Then I moved into a flat.

Drink continued to be a problem. I'm not drinking now, but it's never far from my head. The temptation is always there. I think of the nuns, and want to drink and forget it all. I could never say I'm cured of it, because I'm not.

CHAPTER 52

MARIE

I NEVER TALKED about the Magdalene laundries. Not to my family, nor to anyone else. But about three years ago I was listening to Patricia Messenger who presents *Cork Today* on C103 radio. She was interviewing a guy called Steven O'Riordan who was helping Magdalene women. I rang him and left a message and he got back to me that same day. I told him a small bit of my story and he said I could come to a meeting in Dublin.

'We have one every couple of weeks,' he said. 'And there's one coming up next Friday. Can you come to that?'

On the day I got the train into Heuston Station. A group of women got on at Mallow, and another one joined them at Limerick. They were chatting and seemed to know each other well.

When I got off the train, I approached them and asked where was the Burlington Hotel.

'The Burlington? Oh. We're heading up there,' said one, introducing herself as Elizabeth. She looked at me, her head on one side, and said, 'You're not, by any chance, going to a meeting there?'

I said I was.

'Forgive me asking,' she said, 'But were you in a Magdalene laundry?'

'Yes. Why, were you?'

'We all were. We're going to the meeting too.'

They asked me where I'd been and when, and one or two were in the Good Shepherd a bit before me. That made me feel great – it was like I belonged.

When we arrived at the Burlington we were directed to a private conference room. There were lots of women of all ages already there, sitting round a table, and a young man was running around with a clipboard, taking everyone's names. I realised it was Steven. I went up and told him who I was.

I was surprised that he was so young, but I was very taken with him. When everyone was there he spoke to us, and said he would help us all. He would make sure we had all the support we needed.

'I will stand by you,' he said. 'Never forget that. All you have to do is pick up the phone. I might not answer. I don't even lift the phone when my own father rings me, and it might be two or three days before I get back to him.'

We all laughed at that.

'You will probably have to leave a message, and if you catch me at a busy time it could be two or three days before I ring back, but I promise you, I will always get back to you.'

And he does. Always. That's the thing about Steven.

I didn't tell my story. Not then. I sat back and listened to other people. It was good to know that there were other women with lives like mine. Then Steven warned us not to repeat anything we had heard.

'You must never tell the stories you have heard from other women,' he said. 'Not to anybody. That's important. And you can be sure that nobody will repeat your story. It all stays within these walls.'

After the meeting we went to the bar and had tea and sandwiches. And we all chatted. That was nice. I continued to go to meetings. It's been good, keeping up with the other women. Seeing them regularly does help. There are a couple of women in the group who are the same age as me, but I find myself drawn to the older ones. I get on well with Diane and Marina. And with Kathleen, who lives in England. She wasn't well the last time she was over. She is lovely! She's a real lady.

Last year I told my boys about the laundry. I didn't give them the whole story. I just said, 'When I was young I was put in a convent by your grandfather. It was a Magdalene laundry.'

They were was okay about it at the time, but I don't know what they were thinking deep down. We haven't spoken about it since.

Two years ago I met Pat. He's another truck driver, and he's away a lot. He's been so kind to me, and he's put up with so much. I know I'm not good company when I'm down. And I am depressed so much of the time. I keep expecting him to leave.

'Pat,' I say. 'You don't have to put up with me. There's a door there. Don't let me hold you back.' I've nothing really to offer him. After all I've been through sex is out of the question. I can't handle it. And he accepts that.

A few weeks ago I had a breakdown. It wasn't the first time I have tried suicide. This time I had 170 tablets ready. But before

I took them, I rang Susan; she's the nurse on the team at the hospital at Sarsfield Court. She rushed round to see me.

She was pleased with me. She said, 'That's a turning point.' The other times I tried to kill myself I took the pills before I asked for help. She said, 'It's great that you reached out. I'm very, very proud of you.'

I trust Susan. She has been so good to me, always. She has made all the difference.

I think about what happened in the laundries every single day. And I don't just blame the nuns. I suspect other people knew about the laundries. I can't help but feel that the families knew and the politicians – I strongly suspect that the whole lot of them knew. And I blame them all.

I blame my mother and father for not standing by me, but I blame the neighbours too. It was for their sake I was put in Bessborough. It was all down to shame. What if the neighbours found out that you had disgraced your family?

I blame my grandfather for robbing me of my childhood. But I blame myself the most. Everything that happened to me is my fault. Because I let it happen. It was my fault that I went to the nuns. If I had behaved myself I would not have been there. And it was my fault I lost Paul Anthony.

'Ah no, Marie. You were young, and those nuns were bitches,' Diane said, as I finished my story. 'You kept Johnny. It would have been so easy not to.'

And I thought, *Yes that's true*. I can't regret that I had all my babies. I am proud of that. Some would have gone to London for an abortion. I couldn't. I'm not a bleeding Catholic anymore, but I believe in the sanctity of life.

Then Justice Quirke thanked me. He said, 'I know it's been difficult, Marie, but you've done really well.'

There were more women to go after me, but I was exhausted. I left the room, and sat by myself. Things were swimming around my head. I sat there and cried, and cried.

It had been hard telling my story, but it is so important that we *do* tell. Then we can make sure that nothing like it ever happens again. We were orphans or had been abused, we had nobody, we needed help. The last thing we needed was punishing. But that's what we got.

There was so much hurt in that room. There has been so much hurt in this so called beautiful country, and it's all locked behind the door. Pushed away. Sometimes, I think it would have better if someone had put me in a bucket of water when I was a baby and drowned me, like a kitten.

I was thinking that as I was sitting there, and I went on crying and crying. I just couldn't stop. After a while the women came out from talking to Justice Quirke and they saw me there. Elizabeth brought me some tea.

I drank it, and tried to pull myself together. Then I looked at my watch, and said, 'I have to go, or I'll miss the train.'

'But you can't go home,' said Marina. 'Not in that state, you can't.'

'But I have to. I've nowhere to stay,' I said.

Then Steven piped up. 'You, Marie, are not going anywhere,' he said. 'You're staying with the group.'

I protested, but they all agreed. 'We'll pay for your hotel room,' they said. 'You can stay with us, and travel back to Fermoy in the morning.

They insisted. They were so kind. They took me to the hotel, and we all had dinner. And I thought, *This has been a good day after all. For the first time in my life, I'm here among real friends.*

EPILOGUE: MEETING THE PRESIDENT

STEVEN

MR JUSTICE JOHN Quirke's report came out in May 2013. The women were to be compensated for all the years they had worked in the laundry, and were to have pension rights resulting from those years. While we might have wished for more, it seemed fair, and the women began to apply for redress. The total amount of money raised amongst our group of 165 women was in excess of €9m.

Now it seemed appropriate to commemorate all we had achieved in the past eight years. And the best way to celebrate our victory, it seemed to me, was for the women to meet the President of Ireland, Michael D. Higgins, at Áras an Uachtaráin, his residence in the Phoenix Park in Dublin.

I put in a formal request, and to my great delight the president agreed. There was to be a tea party, and the date was set for Wednesday, 3 July 2013. All our group, the Magdalene Survivors Together, were invited, and I ensured that the invitation was extended to include the survivors from the UK.

Kathleen Legg, thankfully, was well enough to make the

trip; another survivor was due to arrive back from America the night before. I worried she would be too tired to attend, but she said it would take a lot more than jetlag to keep her away.

Some of us met in the Burlington Hotel the evening before and ate dinner. Afterwards the women had a drink or two in their rooms. They were popping down the corridor to each other, saying, 'Do you want to come to my room?' and 'Are you alright?'

They sat there, many of them lounging on the floor, talking until the small hours. There was a lot of giggly laughter. I remember seeing Marina, sitting up in bed with the sheets pulled up to her chin. Five women ended up sleeping in a room designed for three.

I think Diane got it right when she said, 'We're like teenagers, but why shouldn't we be? We hadn't the chance to have girly fun like this when we were stuck in those blooming laundries.'

In the morning we enjoyed a full Irish breakfast, then everyone rushed around getting ready and comparing outfits. Marina was cross with me because I hadn't ironed my shirt. 'Give it here,' she said, whisking it away. 'If there's one thing I'm good at it's ironing!'. I wondered if she was remembering all those years she spent pressing clothes in the Good Shepherd laundry in New Ross.

Nancy arrived in time for a sandwich lunch. Alan had driven her up from Galway, and Marie came soon afterwards. Diane admired her colourful top. 'I found it in a charity shop,' she said.

The rest of the women were there by 1.30 p.m., and the excitement was mounting. We were due at Áras an Uachtaráin at 2 p.m. I'd ordered a bus from the Dublin City Council for 1.40 p.m. but it was getting late and Kathleen was becoming restless.

As we were waiting, I asked Marie if she was alright. We'd been so worried about her the day all the women spoke to Justice Quirke. She smiled happily and said, 'If anyone had said to me last year, you are going to get an apology, you are going to be in the Áras, you are going to meet President Higgins, I would have thought, yeah, right. Steven,' she said, 'it's unbelievable.'

It felt like the best kind of school trip as we boarded the bus. We sang songs like 'Molly Malone', and 'The Black Velvet Band' all the way, but everyone became a little quiet when we entered the Phoenix Park, turned in through the gates of the Áras and caught our first sight of the residence. 'Isn't it lovely,' said Nancy, gazing in awe at the long white building, with its pillared porch that was once the Vice-Regal Lodge.

We were greeted warmly by two officers from the Irish Army, who led us up the steps.

'This is the Francini Corridor,' said one of the officers, linking arms with Kathleen, and leading her to the main reception room. She hung on to him, gratefully.

'I'm feeling a little shaky,' she said, explaining that she had recently been treated with radiotherapy. The officer then found her a chair, as she was worried she wouldn't manage to stand with the others until President Higgins arrived.

'In a while the president will come out, Steven,' said the officer. 'He will shake your hand, and ask you to introduce him to each of the women.'

'That's grand,' I said.

'Then you can say a few words, then the president will make a speech welcoming all the women. And then,' he said, 'it will be time for tea.'

We stood in a circle, along with the group from London who had arrived before us. I gazed at the enormous room, with its distinctive patterned carpet, gold walls and opulent chandeliers. It was hard not to feel in awe of our surroundings, but the women, I noticed, were holding their heads high.

'Just think. The Queen of England was here last year, in this very room,' said Marina, her face wreathed in smiles.

'And President Obama,' added Diane.

President Higgins wasn't in office for the visit of Queen Elizabeth II, or the Obamas. The honour of receiving those distinguished guests fell to President Mary McAleese. But it seemed appropriate to me that it should be him welcoming the women. Being older, he could identify with their stories so well, and grant them solace.

'Look at those flowers, Steven!' said Nancy, indicating a substantial arrangement placed below a mirror. 'Just think. They were put there especially for us.'

I noticed tears in Kathleen's eyes. 'I didn't think I'd be here to see this, Steven,' she said. 'I thought the cancer would have got me by now. And I can't help thinking of the survivors who didn't make it. And who aren't here today.'

There was a hush then, and President Higgins swept into the room followed by his wife, Sabina.

'Isn't she lovely in her lilac jacket,' whispered Marina. And I laughed and agreed, because the jacket Marina was wearing was almost identical.

The president was magnificent. He shook hands with every one of the women and he gave them time to talk. He thanked them for visiting him, and said how good it was to see them there. And they loved him!

He took a shine to Esther, one of the older members of our group. He said, 'You are looking lovely today. What a beautiful dress.' He was holding hands with her. We teased her afterwards.

'He was flirting with you,' I said, and she blushed.

'What nonsense! His people came from near where I grew up. That's why he talked to me.' But she couldn't stop smiling.

Sabina Higgins is wonderful in the role of First Lady. She put her arms around the women, kissing each of them on the cheek, showing a genuine warmth towards them. Diane admired her dress, then asked her where she had bought it. And she said, 'I picked it up in Debenhams.'

There was such a lovely festive atmosphere. Everyone was happy.

I then thanked the president for extending such a warm welcome, then he stood up to say a few words. And I was truly impressed. He started by acknowledging the wrong that had been done to the women, and emphasised his distress at the nation's silence on their plight.

'Your story has caused important questions to be asked so as to ensure that such mistakes of the past are never repeated,' he said. 'The lessons from your experience must be learned if we are to create a just and inclusive society, one that is truly participatory, allowing all its citizens a voice and the right to be treated with respect and decency.'

Then he congratulated them on all they had achieved. And I saw them all smile, and stand up just a little bit taller.

'You have shown Irish citizens the value of working together, of harnessing the strength that lies behind a collective to change things for the better. Your courage shows that there are no inevitabilities in life that cannot be transformed by the justness of a cause and the strength of a conviction.'

I caught Marina's eye then, and smiled. This speech was so apt.

'As you continue now on your personal paths through life, my wish for you is that it is with a sense of peace and resolution; and a reassuring knowledge that a society that once let you down so badly has now embraced you, and the many other brave women who are part of the Magdalene story, in their hearts, and in their conscience, too.'

His speech was greeted with rapturous applause, then there was a brief silence. I looked round the group and saw tears behind the smiles. And they were tears of joy.

Kathleen pulled on my sleeve. 'Steven,' she said. 'Do you remember that day we first met?' I said I did. 'You were so young,' she said, 'I did wonder if you would be any help to me.' She paused to wipe her eyes. 'I can hardly believe we have come so far. Thank you for sticking by me and being true to your word.'

I held her hands in mine, and a tear came to my eye, too. I was as fond of Kathleen as if she was my grandmother, and I had been so worried that she would die without her story being told. This seemed the best possible ending.

We moved through to the state dining room, where a magnificent tea was laid out. Nancy, Marie and Marina fell on it, filling their plates with sandwiches, pastries and cakes. I noticed Sabina Higgins walking Kathleen through to where one of the army officers had placed a chair. They were deep in conversation.

Sitting her down, Sabina said, 'Prince Charles sat where you're sitting.' Then a waitress arrived with a plate full of gluten-free treats for Kathleen. She smiled, gratefully. Nothing was too much trouble at the Áras that day.

The formalities over, the atmosphere relaxed further. And, eating that wonderful spread, the women's joy seemed complete. 'It's been the happiest day,' they said. 'The best day ever. We feel so welcome.'

All too soon it was over. Photographs taken, goodbyes said,

it was back to the bus. But that wasn't quite the end. There was the promise of a celebration dinner.

But first, there was the media to think about. Joe Little of RTE jumped onto the bus and asked some of the women what they thought of the day. One woman who talked to Joe, Kathleen Whelan, was still in an institution. The nuns had forbidden her to come to see the president, but she had come anyway, and now she wanted to share her story.

'I defied those nuns today,' she said, proudly. 'And I'm glad I did. I'm so happy I came. I wouldn't have missed meeting the president for the world.'

Others echoed this sentiment, and the clips of them were beamed round the world in the news. But it was perhaps best summed up by Marina.

'Being a Magdalene woman was awful,' she said. 'But a lot of good has come from this. We've met some wonderful people. We would *never* have met the Taoiseach or the president but for this. But more important, we've made some good friends. And we all love each other. We might sometimes have words, but we *do* all love each other and we look after one another.'

The press conference over, the bus started its drive back to the hotel and I suggested we sing another song.

'Does anyone know "Whispering Hope"?' asked Diane.

'I do!' One of the survivors took out a harmonica, and started to play. And all the women raised their voices in song.

> When the dark midnight is over,
> Watch for the breaking of day.
> Whispering hope, how welcome thy voice,
> Making my heart in its sorry rejoice.

ACKNOWLEDGEMENTS

The creation of this book is not just down to one person or one idea. It is about a group of people working together and creating a process that breathes life into a story they wish to tell.

To this end *Whispering Hope* was only made possible thanks to a few good people. They did not just believe in the story, but wanted to tell the world about it.

These include the wonderfully talented ghost writer Sue Leonard. Ghost-writing is not just a skill but an art-form and without Sue's commitment, vision and determination for this book it would not have been possible to complete it.

To our agent Mulcahy Associates and in particular Sallyanne Sweeney, we want to say a massive thank you.

To our wonderful publishers Orion and the extremely talented Anna Valentine who not only helped us shape the book but allowed us free will to create what we envisioned. Thank you! Your trust and the trust of our agent has allowed us to excel and achieve beyond imagination.

For years Magdalene survivors have struggled against a wall

of silence that could not be broken. We hope that *Whispering Hope* not only tears down those walls but allows the story of these women to be told to a wider global audience.

To our family and our friends, to people we have met along the way and to those who supported us and marched with us, we say 'thank you', because without your support, your help, guidance and solidarity, the story of the Magdalene laundries might well have been consigned to the pages of a different sort of history.

And finally to the women, all the women, from all the institutions, this is for you because you need whisper no more!